MAGNIFICENT MERCEDES

THE COMPLETE HISTORY OF THE MARQUE

MAGNIFICENT MERCEDES

THE COMPLETE HISTORY OF THE MARQUE

GRAHAM ROBSON

Bonanza Books

New York

© 1983 Winchmore Publishing Services

First published in USA 1981
Second Edition

Published by **Bonanza Books**

Distributed by Crown Publishers Inc.
One Park Avenue
New York
NY 10016 USA

Designed by Laurence Bradbury

Produced by Winchmore Publishing Services
40, Triton Square,
London NW1 3HG

ISBN 0 517 405 377

Printed in Hong Kong

Library of Congress Cataloging in Publication Data

Robson, Graham.
  Mercedes.

  Includes index.
  1. Mercedes automobile – History. I. Title.
TL215.M4R64   1983   629.2'222   82-22683
h g f e d c b a

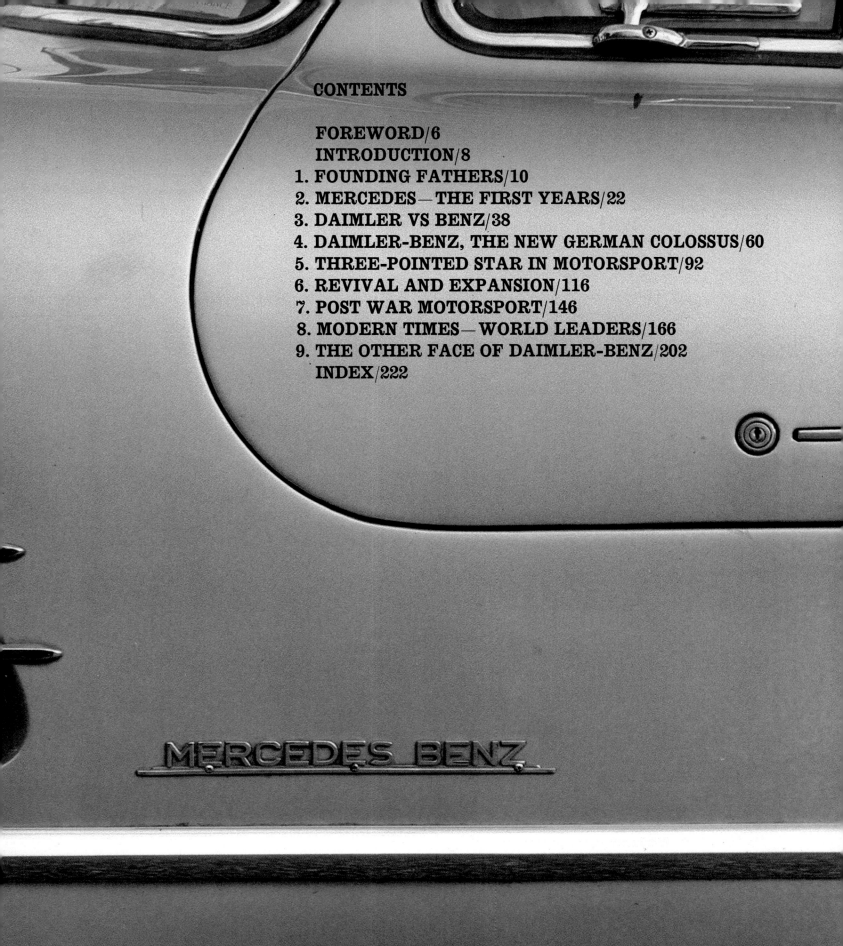

CONTENTS

MERCEDES BENZ

FOREWORD

If we are to believe certain sources, the history of the motorcar goes back as far as ancient China. Others claim that Verbiest, Cuquot and Trevithick, who first enticed steam engines to be less than stationary, were the founding fathers. Sam Browne made a coal-gas-engined carriage in 1824; Siegfried Marcus made a workable car in 1877.

The reason why we acknowledge Carl Benz as the Father of the motorcar is that his car was the first of many. Previous inventors made a ''one-off'' machine and passed on to something else. Benz made a practical vehicle which was intended to be the first of many. This was the difference, a difference in long-term intent.

Gottlieb Daimler was not essentially a ''car'' man. He was an ''engines'' man. He envisaged his lightweight, fast-running portable motor as powering all sorts of things. His first application of his power unit was in a motorcycle, next a carriage, then boats. His early financial success came from launches and tugs. Fire engines—the pumps were motorized, not the vehicles, at first—streetcars, sleds, taxis, all attracted his attention. He did not design a car from scratch as Benz had done but put his ubiquitous engine into a horseless carriage. Only later did he and Maybach progress backwards into automobile design.

Thus Benz and Daimler are the men who are universally recognized as the parents of the motor industry. They did not *invent* the motorcar any more than they invented the internal combustion engine (although there is evidence to suggest that had Otto not been the boss and Daimler the Technical Director, the Otto-cycle might have been known as the Daimler-cycle). These two far-sighted, essentially practical men took the inventions of others and with vision and sweat and faith founded an industry.

There is a kind of dramatic rightness that the two parent firms should eventually have merged. Fortunately the motorcar had become legitimate long before its parents married. The infant did have its tribulations; allegedly Benz's first customer was said to be mad to buy a car—and proved it by shortly afterwards being admitted to an asylum. The weaning of the infant was solely achieved by the patronage of the wealthy and aristocratic. The car first gained acceptance as the rich man's toy, gradually taking the place of the blood-stock horses and sporting curricles in his stableyard. The future of the car was not really assured until it became a sporting animal. The horse survives today largely so that it can compete. The car, by racing, established itself in the sporting calendar, and was thereby prevented from becoming a mere passing fad.

The early history of the car is closely tied in with racing. In those days, there was no ''GT,'' nothing ''modded'' or ''breathed on.'' Every and any car could race or hill climb and thus racing success sold a lot of cars. Competitive success achieved by some way-out designer's nightmare at Le Mans nowadays seldom if ever brings a modern manufacturer. In those days a car was a car was a car—you raced it one day and took the family out in it the next.

Graham Robson has produced an interesting book which fits in neatly between the ''history'' books and the ''picture'' books. Such a compression can squeeze out much material but he has edited his sources wisely and his omissions are justifiable and in some cases laudable. Having been involved in matters Mercedes for many years I found little to carp at and much to praise.

Graham Robson's last chapter is most important as so few books on Daimler-Benz ever mention the fact that the firm is the largest motor manufacturer outside of the USA on account of its commercial, marine and railway involvement. Another satisfactory completion of the circle is made when you realize that the railway engines are now made in the factory Maybach founded when he left DB. In recent years, the company has concentrated more and more on increasing its penetration of the commercial vehicle market—to use the jargon of the trade. This does not mean that the cars have been ignored, far from it—as Chapter 8 demonstrates. I imagine no other manufacturer spends so much on research and development. However, gradually, the company is ceasing to be a ''car'' firm and has become a ''Giant of the motor industry.'' Is this a good thing? It gives them the resources to research and develop, to make the best engineered cars in the world even better. What is sad, perhaps, is that an ''industrial giant'' cannot indulge in ''follies''—as the author points out—no more gull-wings, 600s or other cars that cannot pay their way.

I would like to think it was not too unlikely that once again the Three-pointed Star would dominate on the racetracks of the world but I have a dismal feeling that racing would not be cost-effective or economically viable. Unfortunately for the ardent admirers, those who own or would like to own a Mercedes, those who will want to add this volume to their collection, the considerations of sentiment will weigh little against the arguments of the cost accountants. And when you are selling as many cars as you can make, who needs the publicity?

This book should certainly stand on every enthusiast's bookshelf not only for its excellent photographs but also for its lucid text.

Gerald Coward
Chairman, Mercedes-Benz Club

INTRODUCTION

When Daimler revealed the original Mercedes model in 1901, it caused a sensation and set new world standards in motorcar design. In engineering terms, it was the best car in the world. Eighty years later, the most modern Mercedes-Benz models are the S-class sedans and the SL-class coupes; they, too, are cars which the competition is struggling to equal.

The significance of Mercedes and Mercedes-Benz models is that they have always been as good as this. At regular intervals, new racing or passenger cars have appeared which astronished the world. In 1914 it was the 274.6cu in (4.5 liter) Grand Prix car, in the 1920s it was the Porsche-designed supercharged sports cars, while in the 1930s there was the dominance of Grand Prix racing by the W25, W125 and W154 "Silver Arrows."

After the Second World War came the futuristic 300SL "gull-wing" coupes, the phenomenal W196 and 300SLR competition cars, and the mid-engined Type C111 Wankel-engined prototypes. In and around all this was the succession of fine sedans, trucks, buses, and aerospace products, all built to the same standards and all enormously successful all over the world.

More than anything else, the products have been remarkably consistent. I doubt if there has ever been a bad Mercedes or Mercedes-Benz product – and most have been truly outstanding. The three-pointed star trademark is one of the most famous and instantly recognizable of the 20th century.

The story of Mercedes, however, does not begin in 1901, but in 1886, when Gottlieb Daimler built his first-ever four-wheeler motorcar at Cannstatt, in Germany. By 1890 the Daimler-Motoren-Cesellschaft had been formed and Daimler cars were being sold. Before this, however, the world's first practical gasoline-powered machine – a tricycle – had been built by Carl Benz at Mannheim, also in Germany, and for the rest of the 19th century these two pioneers were direct rivals.

Gottlieb Daimler died in 1900. His successor, Wilhelm Maybach, was persuaded by a wealthy Austrian businessman, Emil Jellinek, to design

an entirely new type of car on more advanced lines. The new car was to be ready for the Nice Speed Week of 1901, Jellinek would take delivery of the entire first production run, and he also chose its name. Emil Jellinek was the fond father of a beautiful daughter. Her name, and that of the new car, was Mercedes.

The brand-new four-cylinder Mercedes swept the board at Nice. It was faster, lower, more flexible, and had better handling than any of its rivals – almost overnight it made all existing designs obsolete. In a couple of years there were no more Daimlers as all the company cars were called Mercedes, and only a disastrous factory fire in 1903 could halt their progress. After a move of only a few miles, from Cannstatt to Unterturkheim, in Stuttgart, the advance continued.

Benz, in the meantime, was struggling, with outdated designs and a stubborn founder. It was not until the end of the 1900s that the balance was restored. From then until the mid-1920s, the Mercedes and Benz marques fought bitterly for German (and European supremacy.

Both firms sold wide ranges of well-engineered and expensive cars, and eventually both found that the best form of advertising was success in motorsport. Before the outbreak of the First World War, Mercedes cars won the Grand Prix twice – in 1908 and 1914 – while Benz produced the 200hp "Blitzen" car which took and held the World's Land Speed Record.

Until the 1920s the rivalry continued with Daimler and Benz facing each other in motorcar, commercial vehicle and aero-engine design. Daimler was based at Stuttgart and Benz at Mannheim. Both wanted to win the long-term battle for supremacy. It was Germany's runaway inflationary period of the early 1920s, however, that changed everything. Faced with imminent economic ruin, Daimler and Benz agreed in 1924 to co-operate in certain respects. In 1926 they merged completely giving birth to the Daimler-Benz concern and the Mercedes-Benz marque.

In the meantime Mercedes had started supercharging its cars, and Dr

Ferdinand Porsche had joined the company to design a series of new models. Although, for the next few years, there were some worthy but ordinary touring cars in production – some Daimler and some Benz inspired – it was the "blown" K, S, SS, SSK and SSKL models that really made the headlines. Once again the three-pointed star was back in racing prominence, this time with the famous combination of an overhead camshaft engine and a super-charger which could be clutched into or out of operation at the whim of the driver.

In the 1930s, though, Daimler-Benz not only went from success to success on the race tracks, but it brought in a series of technically advanced production cars. Between 1934 and 1939, of course, there was the magnificent period in which Mercedes-Benz (and Auto-Union) cars took complete control of Grand Prix racing. Between 1934 and 1937 the Grand Prix cars had supercharged straight-eight engines, the last of all being 408.8cu in (6.7-liter) monsters with up to 646bhp, while the 1938–1939 cars had V12s of up to 485bhp. Because of their bodywork, they were known as the "Silver Arrows," and they made a mockery of all the regulations hopefully devised to limit speeds and power outputs.

At the same time, the group's passenger cars were transformed. On the one hand Daimler-Benz went purposely "down market" so that it could sell many more cars, and on the other hand revolutionized the engineering used. Out went the heavy, high, crude old models, and in came small, light, low, and technically advanced machines. Daimler-Benz was among the first to adopt all-independent suspension, to produce rear-engined sedans, and even found time to sell a few mid-engined sports cars (the 150H models).

At the same time, there were the 370K/500K/540K sports tourers, with supercharged eight-cylinder engines and 100mph (160km/h) performance and – even more enormous, and exclusive – the Type 770 "Grosser" limousines and cabriolets which no ordinary individual could possibly afford.

Then came the Second World War,

and because Daimler-Benz built thousands of superb inverted V12 aero-engines its factories were prime targets for bombing. By 1945 destruction was almost total. However, it was something of a miracle that rebuilding was so complete and so successful by the early 1950s.

Once back on its feet, commercially and economically, Daimler-Benz carried on where it had left off. It began the 1950s by introducing the new 300 series, a splendid "flagship" which carried on for some years, followed it up by the advanced racing "space-frame" 300SL coupe, which introduced "gull-wing" doors to a startled world, and confirmed its return to technical pre-eminence in 1954–1955 with the sensational and almost entirely successful W196 Grand Prix cars and 300SLR racing sports cars, which shared the same basic design. At the end of 1955, however, Daimler-Benz withdrew from racing, and has never returned to it.

Since then, of course, Daimler-Benz has concentrated on making more, better, and increasingly supreme passenger cars, trucks and public service vehicles. Having introduced its first pressed-steel unit-construction bo body shell in the mid-1950s, it refined and improved the design, the styling, and the detail with every model change.

There were new overhead camshaft engines, redesigned swing-axle rear suspensions, fuel injection, and many other features in the 1950s. Presitigious and sumptuously trimmed cars like the 220SE coupes kept one sector of the market happy, while the "pagoda-roof" 230SL/250SL/280SL sports cars took over from the 300SLs with great aplomb in the 1960s.

In that decade, not only was the original "S-class" range of models introduced, but from 1963 there was the gargantuan and enormously sophisticated Type 600 Limousine and Pullman model. To bridge a marketing gap and to extend sales possibilities even further, a new medium-capacity V-8 engine came along in 1969, while a silky new twin-overhead-camshaft six-cylinder engine followed it a few years later.

Just in case the new Wankel rotary concept became viable and fashionable,

Daimler-Benz carried out a development program. All that we saw of this was the mid-engined C111 research model, which proved not only that D-B's three- or even four-rotor Wankels were the best in the world, but that its 1969 chassis designs were the equal of any currently to be found on the race tracks.

Whereas the 1960s saw a huge proliferation in terms of models and body styles, the 1970s have been dominated by considerations of vehicle safety, of fuel economy, and of keeping abreast of world market legislation. As the 1980s begin, therefore, the Daimler-Benz range is noted for its incredibly safe and sure-footed behavior rather than for ultimate performance. Even so, in recent years, the company has found time to start selling station wagons (the T-Wagens) for the first time, to develop the G-Wagen cross-country vehicle, and to announce that it will be selling a much samaller and more fuel-efficient range of cars in the next few years.

Performance may have had to give away to safety and environmental considerations, but that has not meant the arrival of dull Mercedes-Benz products. There is nothing remotely ordinary, for instance, about a 500SEL S-class sedan with its smoothly profiled and spacious body style allied to a 130mph (208km/h) top speed, and there are few sights more impressive in the roughest rallies in the world than that of a V8 engined lightweight 500SLC coupe battling away with the best rally cars in the world.

In general terms, I am now convinced that Daimler-Benz can make the best cars in the world for the 1980s, just as Daimler did in 1901, and I have no doubt that in the 21st century it will continue to do the same. This book commemorates the exciting first 80 years of the Magnificent Mercedes, and looks forward to the next.

March 1981   *Graham Robson*

1. FOUNDING FATHERS

Daimler-Benz did not come into existence until 1924. However, its ancestors enjoyed links with companies and individuals who were actively concerned with the very birth of the motorcar, and who built the first practical machines. The famous marque of Mercedes, an offshoot of Daimler, was founded in 1901 by which time the Daimler company was well established.

It is now generally agreed that the world's first practical motor vehicle was built by Carl Benz in 1885, and that this achievement was shortly matched by Gottlieb Daimler. Both were German, and both pioneering cars were built in Germany, which gives that nation the right to claim to have fathered the whole business of motoring.

Or does it? There has always been a great deal of controversy on the subject, clouded by a great deal of mystery regarding dates, and further complicated by the real difficulty of defining a motorcar at that stage. Large and unwieldy devices powered by steam certainly ran in the 18th century and some steam-powered coaches even came within sight of commercial success in the 19th century, but perhaps it is fair to suggest that the motorcar as we know it was not a practical possibility until Etienne Lenoir's 1860 patent for the world's first successful internal combustion engine had been capped by Dr Nikolous August Otto's invention of his famous "four-stroke" Otto cycle in 1876. Collectively these inventions made the building of liquid-fuel engines possible —they could produce enough power without having to be large and un-manageable. As a result, two men—Carl Benz and Gottlieb Daimler—working independently, set about producing practical machines which, at the time, were known as "horseless carriages."

Both were already established engineers in the broadest and most compli-mentary sense of the word, both had established their own businesses, both were in what we now know as West Germany, and neither knew about the other man's project. Although it is true that Benz completed the first proper motorcar in 1885, it was only a tricycle. Daimler's first car, which ran in 1886, was a proper four-wheeler. Daimler, for his part, had already completed a motorcycle in 1885, and might therefore be acknowledged as the father of the motorcycle industry. To see how they each invented a viable machine, and how each became a pioneering manufacturer of the new-fangled machines, each must be considered in turn.

Carl Benz was born in 1844 at Muhlberg, near Karlsruhe, the son of Johann Georg Benz, who was an engine driver on the Karlsruhe railway. The father died two years later of pneumonia, and Benz's mother, Josephine, moved into Karlsruhe itself. Young Carl attended Karlsruhe Lyceum, followed by the local polytechnic, and eventually joined the Karlsruhe Maschinenbaugesell-schaft, a factory which turned out foundry work and machinery of all types. By 1870 when his mother died, Carl Benz was 26 years old, and had already changed his job several times. By the time he married Berta Ringer in 1872 he had founded his own company with August Ritter—Benz und Ritter—in a small workshop in Mannheim.

For years the business was tiny and always in financial trouble. It was not until the beginning of the 1880s that a near-penniless Benz began to make and sell a few two-stroke gas engines. The company became the Gasmotorenfabrik of Mannheim in 1882 but was still not a success. Eventually Benz cut himself loose in an attempt to start again. Two business friends, Max Rose and Friedrich Esslinger, financed him in a new company, Benz und Cie, and finally, in the winter of 1883/1884, he began to develop his engineering ideas, which now included harnessing the power of an internal combustion engine to a carriage of some sort.

Previous page: Upright Victorian styling on a single-cylinder 1901 Benz. The advent of the rakish Mercedes in the same year was going to render such cars obsolete.

Carl Benz (above). Right: The original Benz tricycle set the world on the way to a motorized 20th century. The single cylinder engine produced less than one horsepower.

1885 Benz Tricycle

Engine: Single cylinder, horizontally mounted, fore-and-aft in frame, with exposed vertical crankshaft and flywheel. Water-cooled. Bore and stroke, capacity: 4.56 × 6.30in, 103.2cu in (116 × 169mm, 1691cc). Two valves, single cam operating exhaust valve by rockers and levers and offset pin in cam-end face operating inlet slide valve. Benz surface carburetor. Maxi-mum power: (approx) 1.5bhp at 250/300rpm.

Transmission: Belt drive from flywheel to differential and cross-shaft, all in unit with engine. Final drive to rear wheels by chain. Release of direct drive (no step-down gears provided) by pulling belt-control arm to neutral position. Engine mounted behind seats and in front of driven rear axle.

Chassis: Separate tubular chassis frame. Three wheels, single front wheel mounted and controlled in bicycle fashion. Cog-and-twin rack steering between vertical steering posts of front wheel and steering column via drag links. Front wheel suspended by full-elliptic leaf spring and radius arms. Rear suspension by full-elliptic leaf springs. No dampers. Rear wheel transmission brakes operated by belt-control lever. Center-lock wire wheels and solid tires.

Dimensions: Wheelbase: 4ft 9.1in (1.45m). Unladen weight: 585lb (265kg).

Gottlieb Daimler's "horseless carriage" — was probably the world's second motorcar. His name lives on as part of the title of Germany's most prestigious maker of cars.

Benz, of course, having no precedents on which to draw, had to invent his own layout in every detail. He, and he alone, had to decide if the front or the rear wheels should be driven, where the engine should be placed, and how many wheels the "car" should have. His original design had a light tubular frame with twin rear wheels, both driven, and a single front wheel which was steered by a lever and complex linkage. The engine was a horizontal, water-cooled, single-cylinder four-stroke design with electric ignition, which produced about 1.5bhp at 250 to 300rpm, drove the rear wheels by way of belt drive and chain, and incorporated a differential gear. The engine itself was behind the two seats, above and behind the line of the rear wheels, and could propel the machine at a speed of about 10mph (16km/h).

Construction took a long time, and although the precise date of the first trial is not known, it is certain that the car moved around the ground surrounding Benz's workshops in the spring of 1885. By the summer of 1886 it was often to be seen in the streets of Mannheim, and before long Benz had arranged to put replicas of this tricycle on sale. By 1888 he had attended the Munich Exhibition, and a year later one of his cars was on show at the World's Fair in Paris.

The Benz, however, really came to fame in 1888 when, to prove that the car was practical and that women could deal with it, Frau Benz and her two eldest (teenage) children took the car away from Mannheim while Benz was

still asleep, and drove it, with several stops along the way, from Mannheim to Pforzheim, thus completing the first-ever long-distance journey in a motorcar. Five days later, with a minimum of fuss, the party returned to Mannheim.

Benz's rival, Gottlieb Daimler, was born in 1834, the second of four children fathered by Johannes, who was a baker in the little Swabian town of Schordorf. In 1848 the young Daimler was apprenticed to a gun-maker, later moved on to a polytechnic, and in 1853 began work at the Werkzeug Maschinenfabrik in Grafenstadt near Strasbourg. After three years he went off to the Stuttgart Polytechnic, graduated in several engineering subjects with honors, and by 1859 he was back at Grafenstadt, this time working for Messner, who built steam locomotives.

Daimler, however, seemed to be a restless soul and there were to be several jobs in the next decade or so before he was appointed technical director of the new Deutz Gas Engine Works of Otto und Langen in Deutz, but in the meantime he had also met and made a lifelong friendship with Wilhelm Maybach, who was eventually to be the designer of the very first Mercedes car. Daimler's marriage to Emma Kurz, incidentally, had taken place in 1867.

Once established with Otto und Langen, whose founder was, of course, the inventor of the four-stroke internal combustion engine, Daimler saw to it that Maybach was appointed chief draftsman. However, his ten years with the concern, building and developing bigger and better stationary engines, is best described as stormy. After one final and definitive argument, Daimler left the firm, moved his family to Cannstatt in Swabia, and set up his own workshops, along with Wilhelm Maybach, to study high-speed gasoline engines and their possible applications to road vehicles and to boats. This led in 1883/1884 to a patent being granted to Daimler for a high-speed (750rpm!), enclosed-crank, four-stroke, liquid-fuel engine, making the idea of a Daimler "car" practical at last.

So it was that Daimler and Maybach first built a very crude—iron-tired on

This 1888 Benz was the type in which Frau Benz made her historic 92-mile (147km) round trip from Mannheim to Pforzheim without her husband's foreknowledge.

wooden wheels—motorized bicycle in 1885, powered by a single-cylinder 0.5bhp engine [16.1cu in (264cc), air-cooled, bore 2.32in (59mm), stroke 3.94in (100mm)], in which the rider literally sat above and astride the tall engine. This, however, was only the start, for Daimler anticipated that if his engines were really good enough in the future, then they would certainly take over from the horses used to draw carriages. Therefore, and with a certain amount of logic, Daimler decided to graft one of his motors into a carriage normally driven by horses, and duly purchased one from a firm of coachbuilders in Cannstatt. Unlike Carl Benz who had designed a complete car from the ground upward, the very first Daimler was a converted carriage, with a single-cylinder engine of 1.5bhp mounted vertically in the middle of the frame, driving the rear wheels through exposed gears. The Daimler had hot-tube ignition, which set something of a precedent, and a crude type of differential gear incorporating slipping leather disks, which did not. Its first journey was completed in 1886, and one of its original short runs was between Cannstatt and Unterturkheim, a location which was eventually to become very important to the history of the company.

It is interesting to note that at this time it was quite illegal for such machines to be used on the public highway in parts of Germany. This meant that use of the prototypes brought both Daimler and Benz into continual conflict with

Before Daimler built his first car, he designed a two-wheeler, the world's first motorcycle, with an engine producing 0.5hp.

The 1886 Daimler shows the mid-position of the lofty single-cylinder engine.

1886 Daimler "Horseless-Carriage"

Engine: One cylinder vertically mounted with cast-iron cylinder block and fixed cylinder head. Air- and water-cooled. Bore and stroke, capacity: 462cc 2.76in × 4.72in, 28.2cu in (70 × 120mm). Two valves per cylinder. Atmospheric inlet valve operated by cylinder suction, and side exhaust valve operated from camshaft on end of short crankshaft. One surface carburetor. Maximum power: (approx) 1.1bhp at 600rpm.

Transmission: Power transmitted to the rear wheels by various sized pulleys from engine to countershaft. Countershaft had gears meshing with sprockets fixed to rear wheels. This shaft incorporated a leather-type differential.

Chassis: Separate steel and wood chassis frame, modified from carriage originally intended for use with a horse and shafts. Open four-seater body style. Front axle beam suspended on full-elliptic leaf springs. Rear suspension of axle shaft by full-elliptic leaf springs. No dampers. Curved rack on front axle and gear on vertical steering column for steering. Hand-operated block brakes to rear tires. Center lock wooden road wheels with small-section solid tires.

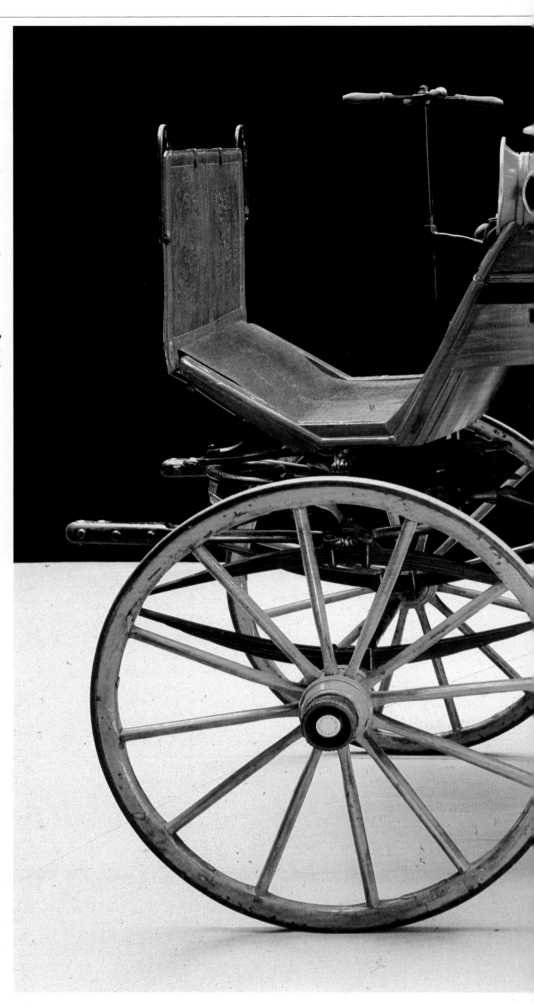

Left: Gottlieb Daimler reclines in the back seat of his 1886 car, with Paul Daimler at the controls. It was the world's first four-wheeled car.

the authorities. It was probably for this reason that Benz's original efforts were mainly directed to selling cars through the agency of Emile Roger in Paris, and that Daimler's prosperity at the end of the 1880s continued to flourish by the building of stationary engines. In those early years, incidentally, Benz became convinced that he ought to be building a four-wheeled rather than a three-wheeled machine, and he made the conversion in 1891, by which time the Roger agency had probably sold less than a dozen cars of all types. It was in France, too, that Daimler made his original breakthrough, for it was in 1887 that Edouard Sazarin, a Belgian, bought the French rights to build Daimlers, and turned to the small firm of Panhard et Levassor to make the cars for him: the first Panhard et Levassor car took to the road in 1891.

In those early days, when virtually all machinery was manufactured and assembled with the help of a great deal of skilled hand work, it was often difficult to define where the one-off assembly of prototypes actually evolved to the series production, however haltingly, of cars of the same type. Benz, indeed, went through another stormy disagreement with his fellow directors at the end of the 1880s, over the time and money being spent on motorcar development, parted company with them, and then attracted the support of two more forward-looking financiers. For a time in the early 1890s, however, Benz concentrated on the production of gasoline-driven stationary engines, but from 1893, when a total of 500 such engines were built in one year, he was able to start building four-wheeled Benz cars in some numbers.

Daimler was hampered by the attitude of the police authorities in his region at first, but orders came in rapidly for Daimler engines for marine and stationary use. A taxi was in service at Stuttgart station in 1888, and Daimler fire engines were also built, not to mention an early example of the engine-powered and propeller-driven airship. By the end of the 1880s Daimler had built a handful of cars, and — along with Maybach — had also begun the development of the world's first twin-cylinder motorcar engine, a narrow-angle ''V''-twin. By then, in any case, he had abandoned his original ''horseless carriage'' schemes. At the Paris World's Fair of 1889 Daimler showed a purpose-built car, complete with the water-cooled ''V''-twin engine. His battle, head-on with Benz, had now truly begun.

By 1889 Daimler had refined his design considerably, and this wire-wheeled example had a 1.65hp engine.

The 1897 taxi-cab produced by Daimler with a 4hp engine, shows that the company was already beginning to cater for all types of transport.

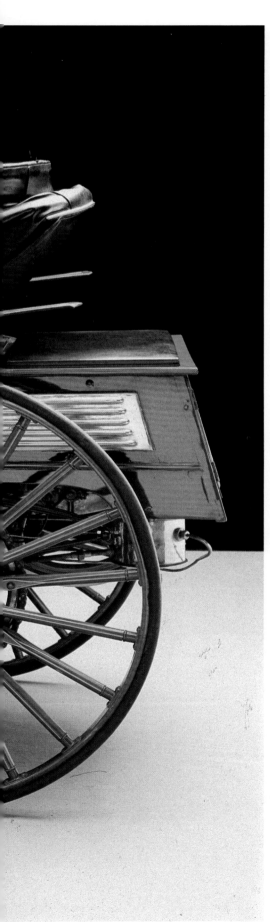

*The 5hp Benz "Victoria" was one of the world's
first series-production cars. This is an 1893
model.*

In the 1890s, therefore, the world's motor industry, which was centered in
Germany and France, began to take shape. The bulky four-wheeled Benz
"Victoria" cars went on sale in 1893, and were soon followed by the smaller,
lighter, and highly effective "Velo" models, which made their debut in 1894.
Daimler claimed that the Velo was the world's first quantity-production car
even though the numbers built were still very restricted. Only 67 Benz cars
were built in 1894, but in the following year, by which time the Velo had
become known, 134 cars were delivered of which 62 were Velo models. Already
the export market was becoming important, for in 1895 Benz und Cie sent no
fewer than 49 cars to France.

Progress at Daimler was held back by the dispute between Gottlieb Daimler
and Wilhelm Maybach, and their partners. Daimler-Motoren-Gesellschaft had
been formed in 1890, but the partnership turned sour in 1892. Daimler and
Maybach set up their own workshops elsewhere in Cannstatt, developed the
Phoenix twin-cylinder engine (and—perhaps more important—evolved the
principle of the spray-type carburetor), and did not make peace again with
their firm until 1895. Thereafter the Phoenix model was put into production,
and license-built engines began to appear in French cars like the Peugeot and
the Panhard which also chalked up its first competition successes.

In the last years of the 19th century, the fortunes of the Daimler and Benz
marques evolved in rather different ways. Benz, in Mannheim, stuck to its
original designs (which included the rear-engined layout to be found on the
very first Benz cars), sold more and more cars every year, and became a
dominant force in the world's expanding motor industry. Production rose to
572 cars in 1899, and passed the 600-a-year mark in 1900. A twin-cylinder,
air-cooled, horizontally opposed engine was made available in 1897 on the
"Dos-à-Dos" model (the engine was actually under the area between the back-
to-back seats). In general shape, however, an 1890s Benz was still something of
a "horseless carriage" in its looks, and would soon look distinctly old-fashioned.

Daimler, at Cannstatt, not only set about modernizing its cars, but found
outlets for its products in other countries. Although the engines went to various
European sources, the design of the complete car was licensed to F R Simms in
Great Britain. Production of "British" Daimlers actually began in 1896 in
Coventry as part of H J Lawson's empire, but by the end of the century the two
firms were going their separate ways. (There is still a British "Daimler" but
it is now no more than a badge-engineered Jaguar, and is part of the troubled
British Leyland empire.)

Daimler, however, had a very eventful time in the closing years of the 19th
century. Not only did the firm adopt the front-engined "Système Panhard"
mechanical layout, but it also began to build more and yet more powerful
machines. It had all started in 1897 with an enquiry for a 6hp Phaeton from an
Austrian businessman called Emil Jellinek, and within a couple of years the
company was building a 23hp model which had the very advanced feature of a
four-cylinder water-cooled engine.

It was all too much for Gottlieb Daimler, whose health broke down in 1899;
responsibility for new Daimler designs passed solely to Wilhelm Maybach.
Daimler, one of the most important of the world's motoring pioneers, died in
March 1900 (he was 65 years old).

In the meantime, however, great developments were in progress. The
inspiration behind the design of an entirely new type of car was Emil Jellinek,
and the name given to that car was that of his daughter—Mercédès.

2. MERCEDES—THE FIRST YEARS

Emil Jellinek was not only a wealthy Austrian businessman, but he was also a keen follower of motorsport. As the Consul-General in Nice for the Austro-Hungarian Empire, and a director of the Credit Lyonnais, Jellinek was a powerful influence in a rich part of the world. He had first become an admirer of Daimler cars in 1897, and thereafter urged them on to bigger and better things. According to David Scott-Moncrieff (whose book, *Three Pointed Star*, was one of the first to relate the history of the marque), "People who knew Jellinek describe him as a small, excitable man in pince-nez who, although a wizard at finance, was, in the matter of motorcars, like Toad of Toad Hall—whatever he had, he wanted something bigger and better."

Once he had bought his first Daimler, he became something of an unofficial agent for the company by selling cars to his wealthy friends and associates. The problem was that Jellinek's enthusiasm (and repeated orders) for more and more powerful Daimlers eventually led to their becoming heavy and difficult to drive. Not only were they heavy, but they were high and had a short wheelbase. Handling was problematical, and this was tragically demonstrated in the 1900 Nice-La Turbie hill climb when Wilhelm Bauer, a "works" driver for Daimler, was killed when his 23hp model crashed. The company, as a result of this accident, decided to withdraw from motorsport.

Jellinek, who joined the board of directors at about this time, did not agree. Although he was not himself an engineer, he was convinced that what was really needed was a completely new type of car, with a much lower center of gravity and a longer wheelbase. Fortunately for him, Paul Daimler (Gottlieb's son) had just completed the design of a small car, which Maybach thought might be a promising basis for a new racing model. Paul Daimler, who had already moved on to manage the new Austrian Daimler concern, had included several new features in this compact little car, the most important of which were that the gearbox and the crankcase were cast in one piece, and that there was a foot-operated accelerator control.

With the support of Maybach, therefore, Emil Jellinek was able to persuade his fellow directors to build a new type of car. He was so enthused with the idea that he agreed to take the first 36 cars to be completed on the understanding that he would be awarded the agency for them in France, Belgium, North America and Austro-Hungary. Since 1899 Jellinek had been competing in motorsport under the pseudonym of "Herr Mercedes," and his final condition on the new project, a romantic one by any standards, was that the new cars should carry the same name—Mercédès—of his daughter, who was then a mere ten years old.

It was a very tall order for the Cannstatt company, who were already struggling to meet the impossibly tight deadline for delivery. The agreement was signed in April 1900, and called for the delivery of all 36 cars on 15 October, just six months later. The theory was that this would allow Jellinek to get the cars thoroughly ready for the Nice Speed Week in March 1901.

Things, however, did not go smoothly, as no amount of overtime and night working could ensure that the order was fulfilled. The first six cars were actually delivered to Nice in January 1901, completely untried (they were delivered by rail all the way from Cannstatt to Nice), and one was hastily prepared for the Grand Prix of Pau to be held in February. It was a complete fiasco—one of the few which the Mercedes name has ever had to bear. In trials there was repeated trouble with the gearbox and the engine, and although it managed to start the race at Pau, the clutch would not work, and the gear lever jammed; retirement was only a few yards away.

What happened next, of course, is part of the Mercedes legend. Several cars

Previous page: The sensational 1901 six-cylinder Mercedes. (Coys of Kensington Collection)

Mercédès Jellinek, daughter of Emil Jellinek, in whose honor the original Mercedes car was named.

R A Collings's beautifully restored 1903 60hp Mercedes at the Prescott hill climb in 1976.

1903 Mercedes 60hp Model

Engine: Four cylinders, in line, in two cast-iron blocks, with three-bearing light-alloy crankcase. Bore and stroke, capacity: 5.52 × 5.90in, 567cu in (140 × 150mm, 9,292cc). Nondetachable cylinder heads. Two valves per cylinder: overhead inlet valves with special annular breathing arrangements operated by pushrods and rockers, and side exhaust valves; both valves operated by single camshaft in side of crankcase. Single up-draft Mercedes-Simplex carburetor. Maximum power: (approx) 65bhp at 1100rpm.

Transmission: Scroll clutch in unit with front-mounted engine, and separate four-speed manual gearbox (without synchromesh) and straight bevel differential in rear of gear case. Final drive by countershaft from transmission to sprockets. Drive to rear wheels by chain.

Chassis: Separate pressed-steel chassis frame with channel-section side members and tubular cross-bracing. Forged front axle beam. Front and rear suspension by half-elliptic leaf springs. No dampers. Worm-and-nut steering. Externally contracting drum brake, foot pedal and mechanically operated, on gearbox countershaft. Hand lever operating drums on rear wheel hubs. Wooden artillery-style wheels. Front tires: 35.8 × 3.5in (910 × 90mm) and rear tires: 36.2—7.7in (920 × 120mm). Open two-seater or four-seater bodywork.

Dimensions: Wheelbase: 9ft 0.2in (2.50m). Front and rear tracks: 4ft 7.5in (1.41m). Overall length: 12ft 3.5in (3.75m). Unladen weight: 2204lb (1000kg).

were prepared, proven, and ready to compete in the Nice Speed Week, where they completely dominated the proceedings. Not only were they seen to be very fast and to have good roadholding, but they were also extremely reliable.

Wilhelm Werner, from Cannstatt, was the star driver, and not only set fastest times in the sprints in Nice and up the 9.5-mile (15.3km) La Turbie hill climb, but also won the grueling 244-mile (393km) Nice–Aix–Senas–Nice road race into the bargain.

The new Mercedes was not only a sensational racing car, but it was technically important in every way. To demonstrate that it was more, much more, than an unmanageable racer, the winning car was fitted out with a comfortable body and four seats, and driven quietly and comfortably around Nice. Compared with the unsuccessful—and lethal—28hp racing Daimler of 1900, the 1901 "Mercedes" was lower, lighter, with better roadholding, and more attractive lines. Everybody loved it.

In many ways the original Mercedes was the successful prototype of every magnificent Edwardian machine. It was one of the very first cars in the world to use a frame with pressed channel-section side members, and was also notable for having the engine mounted directly to it, rather than being positioned on a sub-frame. Not only was the chassis and its suspension lower than ever before, but the engine sat lower *and* further back than usual. There were internally expanding brakes on the back axle, and a hand brake on the gearbox countershaft.

The 364.4cu in (5973cc) four-cylinder water-cooled engine was the most powerful ever built by Daimler—it was rated at 35hp—and was graced with cam-operated inlet valves instead of the less efficient atmospheric inlet valves which were more normal at the time. For the period, the silence and smooth running of this very powerful engine was considered quite uncanny.

The high performance came not only from the powerful engine (35bhp might sound puny today, but in 1901 it was quite outstanding), but from the fact that the race-prepared Mercedes was light, at 2640lb (1197kg). Werner's car achieved 53.5mph (86.1km/h) in the sprints, and his average speed up the Nice–La Turbie hill climb course was 31.9mph (51.3km/h), compared with 19.5mph (31.4km/h) for the Daimler Phoenix car of 1900. In the long race from Nice to Aix and back, Werner covered the 244 miles (393km) in 6hr 45min 48sec, an average running speed of 36.1mph (58.1km/h). In racing guise, the Mercedes looked stark but purposeful (it had only two seats, no rear fenders, and only sketchy front mud guards), but when equipped with a touring body it was considered rakish and extremely elegant.

It must not, however, be assumed that this was a major win in a major event, for the most important European races were the town-to-town races which were now so long that they often crossed national borders. It was, however, an outstanding success at a time when the maximum publicity could be gained. The car was obviously very much faster than any previous Cannstatt product, brought new thinking to the motoring and motor-racing scene, and clearly made every other constructor sit up and think. The Secretary of the Automobile Club de France summed it all up when he wrote, later that year, that "We have entered the Mercedes era."

It was, indeed, the start of an entirely new chapter in the story of the Daimler company, and one which was to catapult it into the very forefront of the world's finest cars. Within months, it seemed, the whole motoring business was buzzing with stories about the new Mercedes cars, and Maybach and his directors soon decided to drop the "Daimler" marque in favor of the new name. Historians will no doubt want to know that Jellinek's daughter always spelt her name "Mercédès," with accents, but that after the name was registered and patented as a trademark in 1902, the accents were never used again.

In the next few years, the original Jellinek-inspired Mercedes racing car itself inspired the creation of a whole new family of cars—racing and touring—and it undoubtedly made every other motorcar manufacturer re-examine his ideas about mechanical design. Then, as now, cars produced by Daimler and its successors were among the most important, and most highly respected, in the world. After the 35hp racer came the 40hp racer of 1902, the sensational 60 Mercedes of 1903 and the rather less successful 90 Mercedes of the same year; the series culminated in the massive 120hp cars of 1905 and 1906. Touring cars developed from the original complex were called Mercedes Simplex, the

Opposite Page:

Top: In the early 1900s cars came in all shapes and sizes.... Center left: ...with most delicately formed bodywork.

Bottom left: Side valves, exposed valve springs, removable valve caps and two pairs of two cylinders on a common crankcase, were all typical of the classic Mercedes engines of the early 1900s.

Center right: The delicate handwork which went into the trimming and furnishing of some Mercedes bodies would have graced any elegant drawing room of the period.

Bottom right: In those days the chauffeur was expected to sit out in the elements while the owners luxuriated in limousine-style comfort behind him.

A Mercedes Simplex model of the type which followed the original Mercedes designs of the early 1900s.

Far left: The detail of a Mercedes Simplex dashboard shows the almost complete lack of instrumentation, and the individual oiling plungers for regular "on the move" attention.

Center: This plaque commemorates a successful run from one end of Britain to the other in May 1975.

Left: In the early 1900s when one had a flat tire, one had to change the tires on the wheels, whose rims and spokes were permanently attached to the rear axle.

Below: The Mercedes Simplex sporting style of two-seater bodywork was typical of many fast road cars produced in the early 1900s.

"Simplex" referring to improvements made to the original 35hp style of engine, but additional cars were also developed using the same design principles. By 1905 there were Simplex models rated at 18/22, 28/32, 40/45 and 60/70 — the first figure referring to a nominal output, and the latter to the maximum output actually achieved by the engine. It was clear that in only a few years, and without any new barriers in technology having been breached, cars had become immensely faster and more powerful, even though in many respects they were still somewhat crude and uncomfortable.

As so much of the motoring business in the early 1900s was closely tied to motorsport and a company's attitude to racing, it is necessary to look at the first few years of Mercedes racing and see how the concern learned from it. During the period, incidentally, the company quite outgrew its original premises at Cannstatt, and in 1903 it re-established itself at Stuttgart-Unterturkheim, and made that its headquarters — a base which has never been changed in the last 75 years.

In their first long-distance race (Paris–Berlin via Aachen and Hanover in June 1901) the new 35hp Mercedes cars were disappointing. Fournier's 60hp Mors won the event, and numerous Panhards also finished ahead of the best Mercedes which, driven by Werner, the "works" racing driver, finished fourteenth. It was, nevertheless, a creditable effort for a company which had not previously contested such a major event. In 1902 the 40hp Mercedes (a slightly improved version of the 1901 35hp model) swept the board in the Nice Speed Week, and, in the 1902 Paris-Vienna road race, Count Eliot Zborowski's car made the fastest overall time between the two cities, but lost the race on a technicality, penalized on a trumped-up charge regarding Customs formalities. New developments, however, were already brewing up for 1903, which were to take the Mercedes reputation to even greater heights.

A large 1904 45hp Mercedes tourer towers above mere modern cars on its way to Brighton in the annual London–Brighton "Commemoration" run.

Not all 60hp Mercedes cars of the early 1900s were fast tourers, as this mighty limousine confirms.

Built to conform to the 1000kg (2205lb) weight limits which applied in certain races and trials, the new car was an extensively lightened and improved version of the original 35hp theme. Not only was it considerably lighter than the first Mercedes cars, but it had a much more powerful 566.8cu in (9292cc) four-cylinder engine which produced more than 60hp, a longer wheelbase, and narrower wheel tracks. Furthermore the engine was equipped with overhead inlet valves (but it retained side exhaust valves) which established a new Mercedes layout for the next few years, and by all the standards of the day it was a high-revving unit, with a peak of 1100rpm.

This, however, was not the peak of Daimler's enterprise for 1903, as the "60" was seen merely as the basis of a future touring car. The *real* racer for 1903 was the massive 90hp model, which shared many "60" components, but which had an enlarged and "oversquare" engine of 775cu in (12,700cc).

Once again, Mercedes cars dominated the Nice Speed Week (Jellinek still thought that a good show at this glittering semi-social occasion was as good an advertising coup as anything that could be devised) with 60hp models, but gloom was cast over the whole meeting when Count Zborowski, driving one of the new Mercedes models, crashed into a rock face on the La Turbie hill climb, and was killed instantly. There was nothing in the accident which could be blamed on the car, for the cause was undoubtedly due to driver error. Legend has it that the Count inadvertently caught his ornamental cuff-links in the steering wheel at precisely the wrong moment.

Six of the new 90hp cars ran in the tragic Paris–Madrid race, and although none was involved in the horrifying carnage which developed on that day between Paris and Bordeaux, none figured prominently in the results. Three of those cars had been intended for use in the 1903 Gordon Bennett Race in Ireland (a race which involved a contest between specially selected national teams), but while they were still being prepared for that event they were consumed in the great fire which devastated the Cannstatt works on 10 June. It was a fire, incidentally, which not only brought the 90hp model's career to an abrupt, but temporary, halt, but it also completely disrupted the factory's production facilities for a time. The move to Unterturkheim, already planned for 1904, was hastily brought forward to get the Mercedes cars back on sale as soon as possible.

What happened next was so enterprising, so remarkable, and so unexpected, that it could undoubtedly have been used in any book of fictional adventure stories. With less than a month remaining before the important and prestigious race, Daimler called back several 60hp models from their private owners, stripped them, and re-prepared them for racing. All the effort was rewarded by a fine outright win for one car, driven by the Belgian, Camille Jenatzy, which averaged 49.2mph (79.2km/h). It was, however, a close-run thing, for two of the three "60"'s retired with broken rear axles—the same failure which had halted Werner in the Paris–Madrid race.

After the great successes and dramas of 1903, it was only to be expected that 1904 would be something of an anticlimax, and so it was. Late in 1903 the man who had co-founded the Daimler-Motoren-Gesellschaft with Gottlieb Daimler, Max von Duttenhofer, died suddenly. Wilhelm Maybach, the engineering

Right: By 1906 racing Mercedes cars, prepared at Stuttgart, were producing up to 125hp and were fearsomely fast. The use of the famous white color is already apparent.

Top: A beautiful 1906 four-seater touring Mercedes with 45bhp engine.

genius behind the new Mercedes cars, had been a close associate of his, but it rapidly became clear that he was not at all in tune with Duttenhofer's successor, Wilhelm Lorenz. At a difficult time it made the conception and evolution of new designs even more problematical and it directly led to Maybach's split with the Mercedes marque in 1907. Because of this clash of personalities, Maybach was excluded from many new-model discussions, and had nothing further to do with the racing Mercedes models produced after 1904.

The strained atmosphere, however, did nothing to help the fortunes of the latest cars. In 1904 the "90" could finish no better than second in the Gordon Bennett Race (this time held in Germany—by tradition, the race was held in the country of the previous year's winning nation) with Jenatzy driving. For 1905 an even more elephantine Mercedes, the 120hp model, complete with 858cu in (14,065cc) version of the original 1903/1904 engine, was produced, and followed the growing Mercedes trend by having a longer wheelbase than the 1904 and 1903 models. All this horsepower, however, was not enough to guarantee success, and in the 1905 Gordon Bennett Race, held in France, the best Mercedes finished fifth.

In the next two years, when Mercedes were still effectively without a seasoned head of the engineering division, and while dissension raged among the staff, the basic design was extended still further, but in the 1906 French Grand Prix (actually, it was *the* Grand Prix, the first of all time) the much-modified 880.4cu in (14,432cc) cars were also-rans compared with the winning Renault, and a 1907 scheme to use a Paul Daimler design of a *six*-cylinder engine came to nothing.

In 1907, indeed, not only did Maybach leave the firm which he had done so much to develop, but Emil Jellinek retired from the board of directors. Maybach, even though he was 61 years old, went on to found his own business which not only made splendid airplane engines but marketed superb, very large cars which were direct competitors for the biggest and best Mercedes models. Jellinek, for his part, was no longer in the best of health. His various schemes, enterprises, and maneuvers had, in any case, yielded him a great deal of money, and he retired an extremely wealthy man.

During the time that the big Mercedes cars were racing so successfully, however, the company was also building up its reputation for marketing fine road cars. By 1906, as a direct benefit of the racing program, there was a range of road cars starting from the 20hp model and culminating in the 70hp model, some with chain and some with shaft drive, but all with one or another derivative of the rugged and reliable four-cylinder engine first seen in 1901. At a time when many cars still looked rather upright and were still too obviously based on the styling of the horse-drawn carriages of the 1890s, a low, sleek, and purposeful Mercedes car had the sort of status accorded in modern times to a big Grand Touring car.

While all this was going on, Daimler's great rival, Benz, had come through a great and potentially destructive period of dissension, not to say confusion, over present and future policy. The problem, at first, was that Carl Benz had something of a conservative or traditional streak in his business make-up. Having developed a successful design in the 1890s, he was loth to make hasty or (in his view) unnecessary changes. The consequence was that, at the turn of

A Mercedes 15/20 Tourer of 1910, owned by Mr H R Timms.

the century, Benz sales had begun to sag. Not only did Benz not want to alter his designs, but he did not want to see his company converted into a ''mass-production'' manufacturer. He was also opposed to any type of motor-racing program, even though success would be a wonderful form of advertising, one of the few which really seemed to impress the wealthy customers of the day. When sales slumped in 1901 from 603 cars to 385 cars, Benz and his sales director Julius Ganss began to disagree repeatedly. By the time 1903 came along and sales had slipped alarmingly to a mere 172 cars, not even Benz

The 1902 Benz Spider (with 15hp engine), though built a year later than the first Mercedes, clearly shows how the Benz layouts were lagging behind at this point.

himself could ignore the collapse. Clearly his cars were badly outdated.

In the meantime, however, Ganss's reaction had been to import an up-to-date shaft-driven Renault from Paris, hand it over to the engineers and, in spite of vigorous opposition from Carl Benz himself, to have a shaft-driven Benz prototype built. That car was unsatisfactory, so Ganss then engaged Marius Barbarou (of the Clement concern) along with a team of French engineers to produce a second car. This design, dubbed the Parsifal, went on sale in 1902, while the old belt-driven Benz models continued to be made.

It was at this point that Benz und Cie almost foundered completely. On the one hand, the Parsifal Benz was badly designed and failed to establish itself on the market, while on the other, Carl Benz and his son Eugen were so incensed by the opposition of the other directors that they resigned from their own firm in April 1903.

Ganss's big gamble had gone badly wrong, for in its 1903/1904 financial year Benz lost half a million marks, and he now faced a totally alienated board of directors. As a result, Ganss resigned, Barbarou went back to France (and to Delaunay-Belleville), and the Benz family returned to take control. Within months he saw a new four-cylinder engine grafted into the shaft-driven car, saw the chassis faults ironed out, and saw the demand leap upward. A year later Benz und Cie was back in profit, and the crisis had passed. One of the most significant personalities to join Benz at this time, too, was Hans Nibel (we will be hearing more about him).

It is important at this juncture to realize that although Benz had been the first to get a practical motor vehicle on the road, it was Daimler who built the first four-wheeler. On the other hand, it was Benz who built the first proper production cars in the 1890s, even though it was Daimler cars which were the first to be licence-built in other countries, and which were the first to make their mark in sporting competitions. Daimler certainly invented the first "modern" motorcar—the Jellinek-inspired Mercedes—and it took Benz until 1903/1904 to get back on terms.

By the mid-1900s, with Daimler concentrating on Mercedes cars, and with Benz now looking ahead rather than backward, both companies were building ranges of rather similar shaft-drive or chain-drive cars, and both had offerings over the same wide range of power outputs. In some categories, notably and obviously at 60hp, they were in direct competition.

By this time, indeed, not only were Daimler and Benz in direct competition —on the roads, in the showrooms, on the race tracks and in sporting trials—but they were simultaneously growing out of their adolescent stage and becoming mature corporations. In retrospect it is quite remarkable how similar events seemed to occur to both concerns at about the same time.

By 1907 both Daimler and Benz had lost the services of their founders and original associates. At Daimler, of course, Gottlieb Daimler had died in 1900, but Wilhelm Maybach had also left to found his own business in 1907. At Benz Carl Benz had returned following Julius Ganss's disgrace, but soon became uneasy again, and finally left in 1906 to set up a new factory with his two sons for the production of Benz-Sohne cars, which were not as successful, nor as long lived. Carl Benz, however, was never forgotten by the directors of his original firm, and received thoughtful financial treatment at the time of the Daimler-Benz merger. He lived until 1929, and achieved the great old age of 85 years.

The two personalities remaining with their firms, who were going to have a great effect on the future of Daimler and Benz, were the chief engineers—Paul Daimler at Daimler and Hans Nibel at Benz. For the next 17 years, with a four-year break during the First World War, Daimler and Benz were rivals on all fronts.

3. DAIMLER VS BENZ

One of motoring's most respected historians once observed that it took until the mid-1890s to make cars go at all and until the mid-1900s to make them reliable. After that, he commented with great relish, they were then made to go beautifully. Although this was rather a romantic generalization about the pioneering era of the motorcar, it sums up the developing fortunes of Daimler and Benz rather well. If not by 1905, then certainly by 1907, both companies had shrugged off the personal and commercial traumas of their youth, had abandoned their original designs, were producing splendid new cars, and were both looking forward to a prosperous and expanding future.

In the next few years, indeed, Daimler and Benz came to offer a series of fast and splendidly equipped cars, consolidated their reputations, and continued to be direct business rivals. Both then had a very active wartime period between 1914 and 1918, which included the development and manufacture of a series of more and yet more powerful aero-engines. Both then struggled to survive the very difficult economic and social conditions which existed for some years in postwar Germany.

In those days, almost any motorcar manufacturer who was anxious to establish his reputation for fine engineering used to compete in the grueling and heroic motor-racing events which were springing up all around Europe and in North America, and Daimler and Benz were no exception. Very rarely, however, did their cars compete directly against each other. In retrospect, it was altogether typical of Daimler that it should withdraw from Grand Prix racing in 1908 after it had won the 1908 event, and that it should return so triumphantly in 1914 after a great deal of practicing and testing. At this period in the evolution of Daimler and Benz, the racing cars and the experience gained with them had a great effect on the production cars which followed them, so this story must cover all types at the same time.

A fundamental change being considered not only by Daimler engineers but by designers all over the world, was to the way in which the rear wheels should be driven. By the mid-1900s many successful cars incorporated shaft drive from engine to separate gearbox, there was a cross-shaft at the tail of the box, and final drive to the rear wheels was by chain; every successful Mercedes model followed this layout. It was also a fact, however, that an alternative and potentially more reliable system involved driving the rear wheels from the gearbox by a shaft, and included the differential gear in the rear axle itself instead of in the tail of the gearbox.

In the case of Daimler and Benz, the situation was not confused so much as complicated and illogical. Benz had jumped straight from belt drive to shaft drive when it had reluctantly started selling Parsifal models, but Daimler had not yet made the change. The 1908 Grand Prix Mercedes, indeed, used chain drive, which was logical in that this car was the final expression of design thinking introduced with the 60hp Mercedes of 1901. Benz engineers, for their part, moved *away* from shaft drive in 1908 when they designed the chain-driven Grand Prix car, and they stuck to chain drive for the phenomenal 200hp models which followed.

On production cars, however, the adoption of shaft drive, usually inside a torque tube, pivoted and located at the tail of the gearbox, was not long delayed; on what might be described as its "bread-and-butter" models Benz stayed faithful to this system, while Daimler started to adopt it for its normal road cars from 1908. Apart from the continued use of chain drive on commercial vehicle chassis for a while, and on the monstrously powerful "Blitzen" Benz, all Mercedes and Benz products had shaft drive by 1914.

Before the first shaft-driven Mercedes road cars began to appear in 1908,

Previous page: This 1904 Mercedes model had a 70hp engine and nothing was spared in the effort to get all decoration and detailing absolutely right. It is a racing car with that one purpose in mind – comfort is not a feature.

This big touring Mercedes was built in 1906 and had a 45hp engine.

Although the hood and supporting framework of this 1906 Mercedes model is sturdy enough, the car would probably not have been used often in this state. The glory of an "Edwardian" car like this was enjoyed when it was used for fast touring in an open condition.

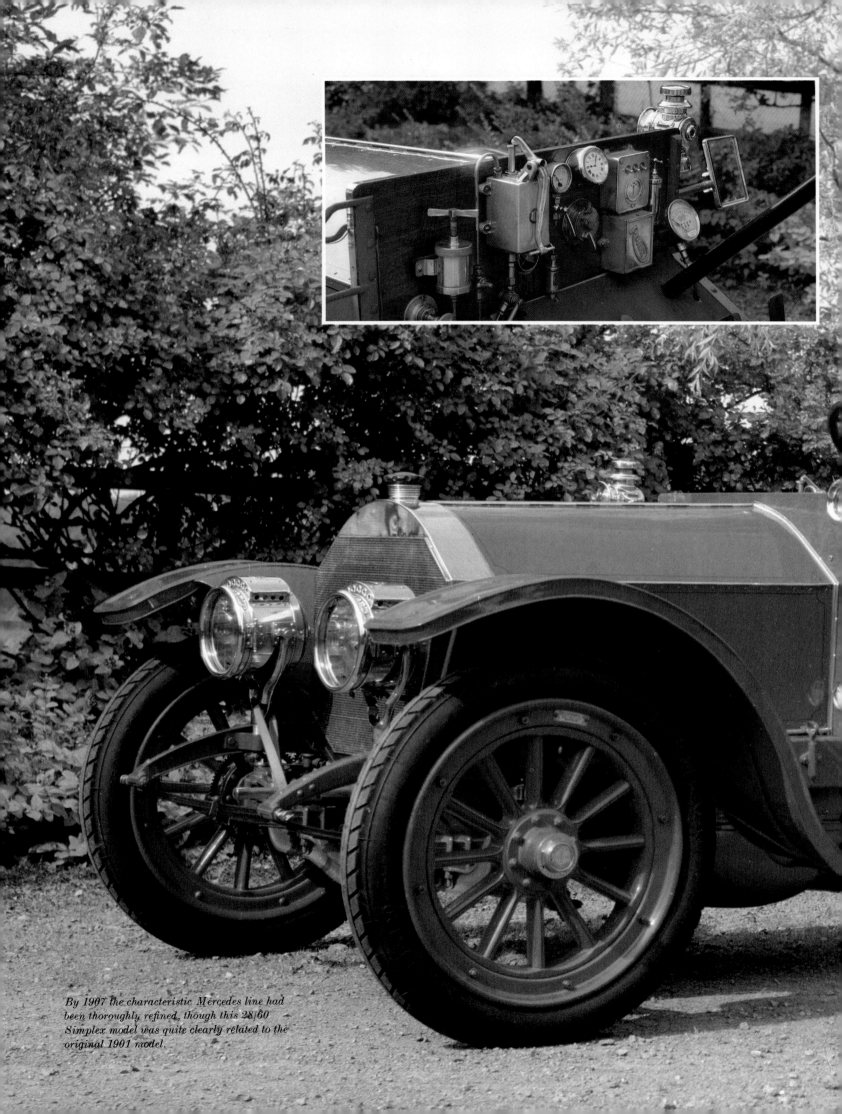

By 1907 the characteristic Mercedes line had been thoroughly refined, though this 28/60 Simplex model was quite clearly related to the original 1901 model.

Top left: By 1907 (this is a 28/60 Simplex model) dashboards and instrument displays were becoming more complex, though weather protection was still non-existent.

Top center: The 1907 Simplex retained chain drive, a feature needing constant attention and lubrication from the Mercedes owner (or his chauffeur), but the first shaft-driven models were about to make their appearance.

Top right: The Simplex models were noted for their simple but enormously strong design details. Front brakes had yet to make an appearance on cars in the mid-1900s, and in spite of the great engines fitted they still had to be started by handle.

Above: This 1908 Mercedes 28/60 Simplex model was equipped with a substantial four-seater touring body. Like many other such cars of the period, there was no direct access to the driver's seat from the "passenger" side of the car.

Left: The 28/60 Simplex engine was still obviously related in general design to the original 1901 engine, though it was more refined in detail. Such engines needed regular attention and lubrication to keep them at their best.

Far left: The noble frontal aspect of a 1908 28/60 Mercedes Simplex with a big radiator to look after the cooling which was not, of course, helped by any engine-driven pump.

however, there had been a significant shift in the sporting fortunes of Daimler and Benz. Daimler (with the Mercedes) began to struggle, while Benz became very competitive indeed. Following Benz's abandonment of belt-driven cars, its newer, faster, and more powerful racing and sports cars were usually driven by Fritz Erle (a Benz fitter from 1894, but chief tester by this time), Victor Hémery (who had been chief of research at Darracq from 1900 to 1906) and — from time to time — by Hans Nibel himself. It was Nibel who, on joining the Benz board of directors, had persuaded them to vote large funds for the development and use of specialized racing cars.

In 1907 success came at once. Erle drove the winning car in the Herkomer Trials (won by Mercedes in the two previous years), while Hémery won the Gaillon hill climb, was second at two other hill climbs and took second place in the Targa Florio.

Both firms built cars for the 1908 Grand Prix, an event governed by a formula which required cars to have a minimum weight of 2535lb (1150kg), and a maximum piston area of 117sq in (755sq cm) — which meant that four-cylinder engines were limited to 6.1in (155mm) cylinder bores, six-cylinder engines to 5.0in (127mm). There was no limitation on the swept volume of the engines which could be used. Mercedes chose to produce the final development of its Maybach-type four-cylinder engine, complete with exposed overhead inlet valves, a 781.2cu in (12.8-liter) unit producing about 135bhp. Benz also chose to design a new four-cylinder unit with a 6.1in (155mm) cylinder bore, which had what would now be called conventional push-rod operated over-head valve gear, displaced 921.4cu in (15.1 liters), and produced no less than 150bhp at 1500rpm. Both cars, as already mentioned, had chain drive.

Earlier in 1908 Hémery had used a similar 120bhp Benz to win the 429-mile (690km) St Petersburgh–Moscow race, averaging more than 51mph (82km/h) over awful roads, during which it often achieved its maximum speed of nearly 100mph (160km/h). This success, and the fact that the Benz was theoretically faster than the 1908 GP Mercedes, made the Benz team favorites to win the 1908 Grand Prix (in spite of competition from teams like Fiat, Panhard, Renault, Itala and others), though in the end it was the number of flat tires suffered by all the cars which decided the result. All Grand Prix cars were, by then, much too powerful for their tires, and the rough condition of the Dieppe circuit (public roads closed especially for the occasion) helped make the situation worse. Christian Lautenschlager eventually won the race for Mercedes, averaging 69mph (111km/h), with the Benz cars of Hémery and Hanriot in second and third place, whereupon Daimler announced its withdrawal from motorsport, and left the German field to Benz.

There was no Grand Prix racing after this until 1911, by which time Benz was out of contention, but by which time the firm had developed one of the most remarkable racing cars of the day — the "Blitzen" Benz. Existing 1908-type Grand Prix Benz models had already set several records in North America during 1909 — David Bruce-Brown setting a 10-mile (16km) mark at Daytona Beach at 115mph (185km/h), and Barney Oldfield taking the world's record for the standing start mile at 43.1 seconds at the Indianapolis track. At the Brussels "World Championship" meeting in October 1909, however, Victor Hémery appeared in the first of the Blitzen models, was fastest of all, and beat a 1908 Grand Prix Mercedes by a large margin.

The Blitzen Benz was a monster in every sense of the word. Its chassis was conventional enough — even a touch behind the times in that it used chain drive — but it was distinguished by a huge 1312cu in (21.5 liter) engine [7.3 × 7.9in (185 × 200mm) bore and stroke] which produced 200bhp at 1600rpm, and the fact that it weighed a mere 2645lb (1200kg). In other words, the

Blitzen Benz was ver̶y̶ ̶l̶i̶t̶t̶l̶e̶ heavier than a 1908 Grand Prix car, but had an extra 50hp. Its wheels were covered with lightweight "streamlining" disks, and there was a beak-like proboscis above a surprisingly narrow but high radiator shell. Although the body almost looked to be too narrow to accommodate two people, there was indeed a riding mechanic's seat, set well back to the left of the driver's seat. Blitzen incidentally, means "Lightning," which very appropriately described the car's performance, and sounded well with the thunder of its exhaust, which left the engine through stub pipes protruding from the side of the hood.

Apart from its more conventional racing successes — and there were many of

Mercedes might have made the running at first, with its famous "60" and "90," but even it had nothing as dramatic, as powerful, or as impressive, as the huge Blitzen Benz. The Blitzen had only one object in mind : to be the world's fastest racing car, something which it proved on several occasions before 1914.

1909 Blitzen Benz Racing Car

Engine : Four cylinders, in line, in two pairs of two cylinder block/heads on light-alloy five-bearing crankcase. Bore and stroke, capacity: 7.28 × 7.87in, 1311cu in (185 × 200mm, 21,500cc). Nondetachable cast-iron cylinder heads in unit with cylinder blocks. Two overhead valves per cylinder, vertically mounted in parallel lines, operated by exposed pushrods and rockers from a single camshaft in the side of the crankcase. One Benz up-draft carburetor. Maximum power: 200bhp at 1600rpm.

Transmission : Cone clutch in unit with front-mounted engine and shaft drive to separate four-speed nonsynchromesh manual gearbox with remote-control right-hand change lever. Countershaft drive to exposed sprockets and final drive by chain.

Chassis : Separate steel chassis frame with channel section side-members, pressed and tubular cross-bracings. Light-alloy two-seater body shell with passenger's seat slightly behind line of driving seat. Exposed wheels. Forged steel front-axle beam. Front suspension by half-elliptic leaf springs. Rear suspension by half-elliptic leaf springs. Lever-arm, friction type dampers. Worm-and-nut steering. Externally contracting drum brakes on gearbox countershaft, foot operated by two pedals. Rear-wheel drum brakes operated by hand lever and cables. No front brakes. Center lock wire, or bolt on artillery-style wheels. Front tires: 34.4 × 4.1in (875 × 105mm), rear tires: 36.8 × 5.7in (935 × 145mm).

Dimensions : Wheelbase: 9ft 1.1in (2.77m). Front and rear tracks: 4ft 4in (1.32m). Overall length not quoted. Unladen weight 3190lb (1447kg).

them—from 1909 until 1922 the Blitzen Benz was quite literally the fastest car in the world. It took the World's Land Speed Record in Héméry's hands at Brooklands near London in 1909 at 125.95mph (202.65km/h) when such records were established over a single one-way flying kilometer. Barney Oldfield (in 1910) and Bob Burman (in 1911) pushed the "one-way" figures up to 131.27mph (211.21km/h) and 141.37mph (227.46km/h), both being achieved on the beach at Daytona in Florida. All these records, it seems, were set in the same car, which was sold to Oldfield by Benz at the end of 1909, and resold by the barnstorming Barney to Ed Moross for Burman to drive in 1911.

By this time, however, the sporting authorities in Paris had decreed that the Land Speed Record could only be granted to a two-way average speed performance, and Benz's supremacy was rubbed in by the British driver, Major L G Hornsted, who used another Blitzen Benz at Brooklands in June 1914 to set a "two-way" figure of 124.10mph (199.68km/h) which, if one considers the American figures, must have been some way below a Blitzen's ultimate capabilities, but which must also have been limited by the confines of the banked Brooklands track.

Although there was some doubt about the accuracy of Burman's claim (the course at Daytona might—just might—have been too short . . .), there were absolutely no doubts about the meticulously organized and run occasion at Brooklands. Hornsted himself, when later interviewed by Britain's premier motoring magazine, *The Autocar*, said:

"I soon found that on wood paving the engine had so much power that the rear wheels just spun if you even looked at the accelerator too sharply. . . . We got the standing start records for the half-mile at 70.47mph [113.39km/h], and the kilometer at 73.57mph [118.37km/h]. . . . I think that we beat world's records twenty-seven times altogether in this car. . . . . ''

—and all this was with a big crude car designed in 1908!

Nor was the big Blitzen Benz only successful in straight line sprints. It was also a very fast hill-climb car—in 1910 it won the outright prize at Gaillon, defeating Jenatzy's 180bhp Mercedes, and in 1911 Fritz Erle was again fastest overall, this time at an average speed of more than 101mph (163km/h)! On his approach towards the top of the hill, it was written, spectators scattered madly as the gallant Fritz did not seem to be in full control of the projectile. Erle also set the fastest time at the Limonest hill climb near Lyons in France in 1913, his last outing in one of these great cars. In the USA Barney Oldfield used his ex-Land Speed Record Blitzen throughout 1910, subjecting it to the rough-and-tumble of dirt-track and grass-track racing. Although, in truth, it was much faster than any other car in Oldfield's traveling "circus," it never seemed to complain, and never gave other than minor trouble.

Although the 1908 Grand Prix car and the Blitzen were the only types of competition car built by Benz in the last prewar years, they remained competitive throughout, and specially prepared road cars also won long-distance events all over the world. In 1910, for instance, the Moscow–Orel race over very bad roads was won by Isajeff's 60hp Benz, and in the USA the Grand Prix was won by David Bruce-Brown, by one-tenth of a second from Héméry [over more than 400miles (644km)], both of them driving 150hp Grand Prix models. Even Hornsted, who will always be immortal for his 1914 Blitzen Benz drive at Brooklands, used a 150hp Grand Prix type with great success, not only at Brooklands (where it won several races), but in a race in New Jersey. He also set the fastest time of the day on speed trials on Saltburn Sands in England. On the last occasion, incidentally, the car was *driven* (not trailered) the 200-plus miles (322km) from London to Saltburn, and after the trials was

By 1910 Mercedes models were being built with shaft drive, and this 40hp Phaeton was a very desirable and smooth touring car.

driven back again, in the dark, without windshield or headlights!

While all this was going on, Benz, under Nibel, was also developing a comprehensive range of normal road cars. In 1905 Benz advertising claimed that in the previous year Benz cars had been supplied to more than a dozen Princes, Grand-Dukes and Dukes in Europe alone. Between 1908 and 1914, no fewer than 23 different four-cylinder models—shaft or chain driven—and two six-cylinder models were listed. Almost all were known by ratings such as 10/20 or 33/75, which denoted their official horsepower rating, and the actual peak figure developed by the particular engine. Many of these cars were Phaetons, or similar models, but there was a trio of ''Prince Henry'' sports tourers of 25/35, 50/80 and 75/105 inspired by the demand for competitive cars to participate in the annual Prince Henry Trials.

It was the same story at Stuttgart, where the archive shows that more new Daimler models, badged as Mercedes, were introduced in the 1908–1914 period than ever before in the company's history. Technically, however, there was less consistency at Daimler than at Benz, for shaft-drive and chain-drive cars were in production together for some years, and there were two distinctly different types of engine in use at the same time.

Although the first shaft-driven Mercedes models appeared in 1908, this type of transmission was not yet trusted for the safe delivery of really powerful torque to the back wheels. Although the shaft-driven cars, therefore, started with a small 8/18 model and over the next five years were gradually extended to 10/20, 14/35, 21/35 and 22/40 models, the most powerful engine used was the 28/60hp model. All these cars, incidentally had conventional (by Mercedes standards) four-cylinder engines with exposed overhead-valve mechanisms. Between 1910 and 1913, however, a larger and more powerful range of models, the 22/50, 28/60, 38/80 and 37/90 cars were built with chain drive, though the popularity of these cars soon fell away as the world of motoring decided that chain drive was a thing of the past—too noisy, too crude, and needing too much attention from the owner, or more likely from the owner's chauffeur.

By this time, indeed, motoring clients were beginning to demand real refinement from their new cars, and the way was led by cars like the Rolls-

The 1914 21/50 open Phaeton Benz model with simple but well-equipped bodywork and, in the style of the period, exposed exhaust pipes.
(Coys of Kensington Collection)

Below right: By 1914 Daimler and Benz were in open competition in all market sectors. This was a Type 21/50 Benz with an open Phaeton body style.
(Coys of Kensington Collection)

Below: The 21/50 Benz Phaeton with its characteristic "V" radiator.
(Coys of Kensington Collection)

Royce 40/50, and cars from Napier and British Daimler. The secret of refinement, however, was to have a really silent engine; with poppet valves and exposed valve gear such standards were out of the question, but with the new-fangled sleeve-valve engines built to Charles Knight's patents there were great possibilities. In Europe the British Daimler company was first to start selling sleeve-valve engines (in 1909), but the Stuttgart-based company was not far behind. DMG had obtained a license to manufacture sleeve-valve engines in 1909, and sold its first cars equipped with such units in 1910. Between 1910 and 1913 no fewer than four different sleeve-valve Mercedes engines were introduced—10/30, 16/40, 16/45 and 25/65 ratings—the 16/50 followed in 1916, and the last of all was built in 1923, just before the emphasis under Dr Porsche changed to very high-performance cars.

In the meantime, something of minor importance at the time but which came to mean a great deal to a great many people in future years, had occurred —the three-pointed star had been adopted as the company's emblem and trademark. Its history in the Daimler family dated back to 1880, when Gottlieb painted the star on a wall of his house and is reputed to have said: "A star shall arise from here, and I hope that it will bring blessings to us and to our children."

When Daimler started looking for a new trademark in 1909 this was mentioned by Paul Daimler, Gottlieb's son, and was speedily adopted. At first three- and four-pointed stars were occasionally used, but the four-pointed star was soon dropped. At the same time, the accents were dropped from the Mercedes name, though Germans had never used them in any case.

Although no *new* Mercedes racing cars were built after 1908, the cars continued to find success. In 1911, for instance, the Grand Prize of America was run at Savannah, and Ed Hearne's 150hp Mercedes finished in second place. David Bruce-Brown, the American, visited Brooklands in 1912, and won races in one of Gordon Watney's, while in the same year Ralph de Palma took a 1908-type Grand Prix Mercedes to the Indianapolis 500-Mile Race, led throughout, but had to retire near the end when his engine blew. This car, it seems, was brand new, but built to the 1908 blueprints. It proved to be good enough to win the prestigious Vanderbilt Cup (with another 1908-type racing Mercedes, driven by Spencer Wishart, in third place).

By this stage Daimler managers were certain that they had been wrong and ill-advised to withdraw from racing at the end of 1908, for it was quite clear that Benz was reaping the benefit of a successful racing program, particularly with the sensational and charismatic "Blitzen" model. In 1913, therefore, it was decided to make entries in the Sarthe Club Grand Prix, which was not the official French Grand Prix of the year but was held on a previous GP circuit at Le Mans, and to use a whole variety of different engines. Four cars, all with chain drive, were prepared, two apparently being much-modified 1908-type GP chassis, and two being brand new. There were two 457.7cu in (7.5-liter) six-cylinder engined cars, a 543.1cu in (8.9-liter) four-cylinder car with a sleeve-valve layout, and a 564.44cu in (9.25-liter) four-cylinder engine with poppet valves. The significance of this entry was that it represented almost the last use by any manufacturer of chain drive on a Grand Prix car, and that all the poppet-valve Mercedes engines used a single overhead camshaft layout with inclined valves and welded steel water jackets, being virtual replicas of the latest Mercedes aero-engines.

It was no fairy-tale return to motor racing, however, for none of the cars was ever in the lead, which was taken over from the very start by the Delage team which had done so well in the Grand Prix proper. Pilette's car finished third behind two Delages, while his teammates were fourth, fifth and seventh.

A 1913 Mercedes 20hp model, with 183.1cu in (3.0-liter) four-cylinder engine. The roof panel is landaulette style and may be retracted if desired.
(Coys of Kensington Collection)

The 1913 20hp (183.1cu in/3.0 liter) Mercedes shows the characteristic exposed driving position and enclosed "owner's compartment" of the pre-Great War period.
(Coys of Kensington Collection)

Like the 1901 Mercedes, the 1914 Mercedes
Grand Prix car set entirely new standards in
design. It won the 1914 Grand Prix held near
Lyons in fine style.

1914 Mercedes Grand Prix car

Engine: Four cylinders, in line, in five-bearing light-alloy crankcase, with separate forged steel cylinders and integral steel cylinder heads. Bore and stroke, capacity: 3.66×6.50in, 274.6cu in (93×165mm, 4500cc). Nondetachable cylinder heads in unit with individual blocks. Four overhead valves per cylinder, opposed at 60 degrees, operated by rockers from single overhead camshaft. One Mercedes up-draft carburetor. Maximum power: 115bhp at 2700rpm.

Transmission: Double cone clutch in unit with front-mounted engine. Shaft drive to separate four-speed nonsynchromesh manual gearbox with remote-control right-hand gear change. Propeller shaft enclosed in torque tube to straight-bevel final drive. Enclosed drive shafts in "live" axle tube.

Chassis: Separate steel chassis frame with channel-section side members, pressed and tubular cross-bracing. Light-alloy two-seater body shell with passenger's seat slightly recessed and behind line of driving seat. Exposed wheels. Forged front-axle beam.

Front suspension by half-elliptic leaf springs. Rear suspension by half-elliptic leaf springs and torque tube location. Lever arm friction-type dampers. Worm-and-nut steering. Externally contracting drum brake on transmission, foot operated. Rear-wheel drum brakes operated by hand lever and cables. No front brakes. Center-lock wire wheels. Front tires: 32.3×4.7in (820×120mm), rear tires: 35.2×5.3in (895×135mm).

Dimensions: Wheelbase 9ft 4in (2.85m). Front track: 4ft 4.5in (1.33m), rear track: 4ft 5in (1.35m). Overall length: (approx) 13ft 2in (4.01m). Unladen weight: 2408lb (1092kg).

Failure, perhaps more than success would have done, spurred on the designers to greater things, and a start was immediately made on the design of a team of cars to compete in the 1914 Grand Prix. Not only was Daimler determined to win the race, but the company wanted to demonstrate to the world that not only Peugeot could build ultra-modern engines and win races with them. The cars built to do this job were as outstanding in 1914 as the original Mercedes had been in 1901.

In 1914 the Grand Prix formula was very simple—engines had to be no larger than 274.6cu in (4.5 liters), and the maximum weight limit was 2425lb (1100kg). A minimum weight without fuel of 1760lb (800kg) was not likely to be approached by the largest and most powerful cars. However, there was no likelihood of big, heavy, simple racing cars ever again being competitive, for the technically advanced Peugeots of 1912 and 1913 had swept away that concept forever. The 1914 Grand Prix was to be held over 20 laps of a 23-mile (37km) road circuit on the outskirts of Lyons in July, and of the entire entry only one make of car, the sleeve-valve engined Piccard Pictet, did not have an overhead-camshaft engine; most of them were copied from the original Peugeot layout having four valves per cylinder.

If this is all just a little too technical for those Mercedes enthusiasts who are not very interested in the finer points of racing engine design, then the author apologizes. However, it can all be summed up by saying that this development represented a totally new approach to the whole concept of laying out high-performance racing engines, and it brought to an immediate end the viability of big lazy engines with large capacities. It need not be emphasized that the Mercedes engine of 1914 made just as much use of the Henry-designed Peugeot engine as did anything else.

The way in which Daimler tackled its 1914 Grand Prix project set standards by which all future Daimler and Benz racing efforts would be judged. Nothing, it seems, was too much trouble, no amount of preparation and testing was considered excessive, and no expense was spared in exhaustive practice. No fewer than seven cars in various states of readiness were taken to the circuit in France at least three months before the event; drivers, mechanics and a team manager were all housed nearby; and methodical practice took place after which they returned to Germany. A month after the party had left France for Germany, they returned again to Lyons for more testing, this time with shorter-wheelbase-chassised cars, and persevered until the cars were ready.

And what cars they were! Superficially they looked like many other racing cars, which is to say that they had conventional channel-section frames, half-elliptic leaf spring suspension, center-lock wire wheels and narrow two-seater passenger accommodation. The innovations were all hidden away. The two points of major interest were the new 273.5cu in (4483cc) engine and the fact that here was the first racing Mercedes to have shaft drive and a "live" rear axle. The engine, while leaning on all the precepts of the 1912/1913 Peugeot unit, was also strongly related to Daimler's current aero-engines, particularly in the way the cylinder block and water jackets were built up from steel sheeting. The engine had four cylinders and five crankshaft main bearings, could rotate at speeds of up to 3000rpm, and produced 115bhp at 2900rpm. This massive and efficient unit (25bhp per liter was a real achievement at the time) was graced by four valves per cylinder, and had exposed valves and stems. Camshaft drive was by shaft and gears from the tail of the crankshaft. The engine, indeed the whole car, was to the credit of Paul Daimler and his team, and the cars were proudly fitted with "V"-radiators carrying the three-pointed star on each face of the "V."

No fewer than five cars were entered (this was the maximum allowed by the

A splendid and, in a way, rather North American looking, 75hp Mercedes tourer of pre-1914 vintage.

regulations), and their progress was firmly controlled by signals from the pits — perhaps the first time this sort of tactic had ever been applied to Grand Prix racing. During the race itself it became clear that the latest Peugeots were quicker around the circuit because they had four-wheel brakes (the Mercedes cars only had rear-wheel and transmission brakes), but that the cars from Stuttgart were fastest in a straight line, with up to 112mph (180km/h) being available at peak engine speeds. Max Sailer's car led from the start (it was its job to act as the "hare" and to try and outpace the other cars) but, rather predictably, the engine blew after five laps. The Peugeots, driven among others by Boillot and Goux, then led for much of the rest of the race, but Lautenschlager (the winner of the 1908 Grand Prix) took over the lead in the late stages. Boillot's Peugeot expired on the very last lap and allowed two other Mercedes, driven by Wagner and Salzer, to take second and third.

This 1-2-3 victory, with Lautenschlager repeating his 1908 win and averaging 65.83mph (105.92km/h), was so overwhelming, and so humiliating for the French manufacturers in their own country, that it was greeted with silence, even anger, by the French spectators. There was no cheering, and no clapping when the three white cars crossed the line. There must have been not only anger at the sporting defeat, but distaste at the performance by a nation which was already making bellicose political and military noises to France and other nations. One month later, following the assassination of the Archduke Franz-Ferdinand in Sarajevo, France and Germany were at war.

It is worth noting that one of the victorious Grand Prix cars was in Britain when war was declared. It was immediately impounded, confiscated and studied in great detail by many of Britain's most famous car-manufacturing concerns. Another was sent over to tackle the 1915 Indianapolis 500 race

(Germany was not, at that point, at loggerheads with the United States), which it won in the hands of Ralph de Palma, who averaged nearly 90mph (145km/h) around the 2.5-mile (4.0km) oval "brickyard."

Although the First World War was economically ruinous for Germany and resulted in all kinds of sanctions and embargos being applied in the years which followed, it did not result in damage to factories inside the country, as long-range airplanes had not properly been developed. In 1919, therefore, it was immediately possible for Daimler and Benz to start planning for the future, subject to the fact that there were serious shortages of several metallic raw materials and of rubber. This meant that postwar cars from Germany looked rather austere at first, being devoid of much of their brightwork, and they were often sold on bare wheels, it being the customer's responsibility to find suitable tires by whatever means he had at his disposal (which often meant that he had to resort to the thriving "black market") to get his car onto the road.

Although Benz had been kept extremely busy during the war years building not only trucks and related vehicles, but a variety of six, eight and V12 cylinder aero-engines, the company found it very difficult to move ahead during the 1920s. Not only was there an overriding national economic problem, but labor relations at Mannheim were none too good. The result was that Benz's postwar private cars were either developments of a 1914 design (such as the six-cylinder 16/50hp model) or were rather similar and perfectly conventional models built along the same lines. In retrospect, indeed, it is true to say that the most famous Benz-engined car of the early 1920s was *Chitty-Bang-Bang II*, a vast Brooklands car constructed from an ancient and lengthened Mercedes chassis, but with a vast six-cylinder 1153.3cu in (18.9-liter) Benz aero-engine installed—and the strange mid-engined racing "Rumpler" Benz models which resulted from a brief liaison forged in 1921, but cut in 1922 before the first results of the agreement to co-operate between Daimler and Benz became operative.

Soon after the merger of Daimler with Benz, the cars took on something of a "transatlantic" look. No car built in Detroit, however, ever had such a patrician radiator and badge as this 1928 car. (Coys of Kensington Collection)

Edmund Rumpler, working in Berlin, produced his "teardrop" car (Tropfen-wagen) in 1921, in which a six-cylinder engine was mounted behind the driver but ahead of the driven rear wheels, and to which an uncompromisingly streamlined open-wheel body style was applied. It was the world's first mid-engined car (if you discount some pioneering layouts of the 1880s and early 1890s, and caused such an impression at Mannheim that license arrangements were taken out for developed versions to be made by Benz.

Hans Nibel and Fritz Nallinger originally thought that the Rumpler principles could be applied to a range of sports and touring cars, and the original mid-engined Benz prototype had a humble little 10/30 unit of 159cu in (2610cc) behind the driver, and the chassis, incidentally, was fitted with swing-axle independent rear suspension. There were many problems with the proposed road cars, however, so the agreement was terminated in 1922, though Benz went ahead with its own idea of the way that a mid-engined racing car should be built. The result was the 1923 Benz RH (Rennwagen Heckmotor) which had swing-axle front *and* rear suspension, and a special four-valves-per-cylinder six-cylinder 122.0cu in (2.0-liter) racing engine which produced a peak of 90bhp at 5000rpm. (This, however, was not enough to make the cars competitive for the 1923 Grand Prix at Monza, for other unsupercharged engines were producing more than 100bhp, and the sensational supercharged Fiats were more powerful than that.) Although three "Tropfenwagens" started at Monza and two finished the race, they were outpaced, and could only finish fourth and fifth to the supercharged Fiats and an American Miller. Nevertheless, the car averaged 84.8mph (136.4km/h), and Max Wagner, who had been in charge of chassis design and development, was awarded a gold medallion by the organizers for producing "the most outstanding new car in the race." It was, however, the first and the last time in which the Grand Prix cars raced, though two were converted into "sports cars" for events in 1924 and 1925. Historically, however, these cars undoubtedly convinced Nibel and Nallinger that it was worth pursuing the idea of rear-engined or mid-engined production cars one day, and the Mercedes-Benz 130H/150H/170H series of the 1930s was the result.

While all this was going on, the Daimler company at Stuttgart was in a much more healthy and forward-looking condition. To get things moving again after the war, Daimler decided to put the 28/95 model into production, a big six-cylinder car which had been readied for sale just before the war started in 1914. This had been conceived as a successor to the big 37/90 touring car, and was directly inspired by the aero-engined six-cylinder racing cars built in 1913, the 442cu in (7250cc) engine being virtually identical to the DF80 aircraft engine. Prewar 28/95s had had exposed valve gear like the aero-engines and the 1914 Grand Prix engine, but the 1919 model was equipped with light-alloy valve-gear covers. Its chassis was up-to-date rather than futuristic, which is to say that it now had a conventional shaft-driven "live" rear axle, though there were no front brakes for the moment. For general sale to the public, the 28/95 was also joined by the last of the Knight sleeve-valve engined cars, the 16/50, and also by the much smaller and slower poppet-valve engined 10/35.

Even though Paul Daimler and Max Sailer managed to find time to design a sports version of the 28/95 chassis, which had a shorter wheelbase, and looked superficially similar to those of the 1914 Grand Prix cars, and even though Sailer himself overcame all manner of practical, financial, and bureaucratic difficulties to take one to the 1921 Targa Florio where he finished a very creditable second behind Masetti's Fiat, all this was merely a prelude to the great years which were to follow, initiated, in the early 1920s, by the arrival of supercharging and Dr Ferdinand Porsche.

4.DAIMLER–BENZ,THE NEW GERMAN COLOSSUS

It had seemed inevitable for some years that Daimler and Benz would eventually have to come together, or that their continued competition for sales would eventually result in one of them being forced out of business. If the German economy had been stable in the early 1920s, the day of decision might have been postponed for a while, but the whirlwind of inflation which consumed the nation in 1923 destroyed everyone's hopes for the future.

Daimler was in the strongest position to withstand the terrifying financial conditions (where a workman had to bring a suitcase to work to take away a mountain of almost worthless paper money, and where prices of goods were altered daily, or even more often!), and it was Dr Jahr of Benz who made the first overtures, designed to bring Daimler and Benz together.

Talks and formal negotiations began in 1923, and in May 1924 the two firms were able to sign an "Agreement of Mutual Intent" about the future. It was not at this point a complete and formal merger, but it did at least guarantee that the two concerns—Benz in Mannheim and Daimler in Stuttgart—would not be fighting face-to-face for sales of cars and trucks. It was of enormous significance that the new board of management included no fewer than three distinguished engineers—Dr Ferdinand Porsche and Fritz Nallinger from Daimler and Hans Nibel from Benz—and that Wilhelm Kissel became the co-ordinating director of the enterprise.

An early priority had to deal with the problems of duplication. The factory at Sindelfingen, southwest of Stuttgart, which had been established in 1915/1916 to increase Daimler aero-engine production, was vastly expanded and turned into the center of coachbuilding manufacture for the entire group. In the next 15 years, as Daimler-Benz sold more and more cars, and built bigger and better aero-engines, the Sindelfingen plant was enlarged considerably. However, it was not until after the Second World War and after the bomb damage had been repaired, that the chassis and final assembly lines were moved to Sindelfingen. Other very important rationalizations, made to truck, bus and industrial-engine programs, are described in Chapter 9.

On 29 June 1926 the complete and formal fusion of the two groups was made and Daimler-Benz Aktiengesellschaft came into existence. The merger came none too soon, for at the time there were no fewer than 86 different motorcar manufacturing companies in Germany, many making only a handful of cars. And it has been said that one single factory with modern equipment installed could have supplied the entire German market at the time!

One of the first decisions which had to be made, as a means to making the new "image" readily recognizable, was to develop a new badge or trademark. Luckily, both Daimler and Benz had used circular radiator badges for some time, and it was therefore not very difficult to amalgamate the two. Mercedes, of course, had used a three-pointed star since 1909, and Benz had been using a circular laurel wreath for a similar period. It was entirely logical, therefore, that the new symbol should include the three-pointed star inside the laurel wreath—an arrangement which has persisted to this day.

There was also the question of a new name for the cars. In the beginning, in the 1880s and 1890s, there had been the Daimler and there had been the Benz, but from 1901 everything had been confused by the arrival of the Mercedes and the speedy disappearance of the Daimler marque. Therefore, although it was appropriate for the new group to be Daimler-Benz AG, it was entirely logical for the new cars, when they appeared, to be badged as Mercedes-Benz models. Ever since then, for more than 50 years, the company's policy has never changed. Consequently, there has never been a Mercedes-Benz company in Germany, nor has there ever been a car badged as a Daimler-Benz.

Previous page: The aristocratic nose of the magnificent Mercedes-Benz 38/250 SSK model of 1929.

Development of trademarks over the years. Daimler began using the three-pointed star in 1909 and added the ring, name and extra stars from 1916. The three-pointed star atop the radiator was adopted in 1921 and, following the merger with Benz (in 1926), the laurel wreath and the new marque name made their appearance.

However, in spite of the fact that Daimler and Benz teams had begun working together in 1923, well before the formal merger took place, and even though the new group really had too much factory space at first, there was no immediate and savage change or rationalization of the cars being built. The chassis assembly lines at Mannheim (the Benz factory) and at Stuttgart-Unterturkheim (Mercedes) were both kept in use. This situation persisted for some years, and it was not until late in the 1930s that Mannheim was given over entirely to component manufacture and to the final assembly of trucks and buses, while Stuttgart-Unterturkheim became the center of final assembly of all Mercedes-Benz passenger cars.

Before going on to review some of the most famous and significant cars which emerged from Daimler-Benz in the 1926–1939 era, one must attempt to sort out how the model range and model policy were steadily developed. In 1926 after the merger, production of existing Benz models was restricted to the 10/30 and the 16/50 six-cylinder cars, and there was no immediate change to the supercharged 244.1cu in (4.0-liter) and 366.1cu in (6.0-liter) Mercedes models. All the development of glamorous new models was concentrated on the Porsche-designed six-cylinder Mercedes sporting cars. However, at the same time, the development of two new ranges of mundane middle-class touring cars—the "Stuttgarts" and the "Mannheims"—was brought forward. (Those model names, incidentally, denote the factories in which chassis and final assembly took place.)

Later, to build up production without losing any of the sporting image which had so successfully been established in the 1920s, a whole series of four-cylinder and six-cylinder quantity-production cars with side-valve engines was evolved. In these cars technical innovations came thick and fast, including the adoption of front- *and* rear-wheel independent suspension, tubular backbone chassis frames, the use of a diesel-powered engine, and even the offering of a range of rear-engined chassis. During the same period, too, three entirely different straight-eight-cylinder chassis were produced, one having a side-valve engine, and the others having overhead valve designs with superchargers operable at the driver's whim. It must be remembered that, at this same time, the company was heavily involved in motor racing either with sports cars or with out-and-out Grand Prix cars, but this effort is covered in another chapter. It was a wonderfully extrovert way of building up the fortunes of the new group, and it succeeded in bringing Daimler-Benz into the very forefront of technical and industrial reputations.

The most exciting Mercedes-Benz products of the late 1920s, of course, were the supercharged six-cylinder models, all of which evolved from the original 1924 design which Doctor Porsche had produced, and which had originally been rated at 100hp without the supercharger engaged, and 140hp with it working. It is interesting to note, however, that although derivatives of this big engine and its related chassis were on sale until 1933, Ferdinand Porsche himself left Daimler-Benz in 1928 after a blazing disagreement over policy, and handed over all technical responsibility to Hans Nibel.

Although the original Type 24/100/140 was most emphatically not a racing car and not even a chassis specifically designed for sports-car use, all the technical quality and potential were there for everyone to see. Indeed, its light-alloy cylinder block, overhead in-line valves, and overhead camshaft which operated the valves through the medium of finger followers, all set the pattern and layout of many other Daimler-Benz engines which would be built in the next generation.

From the original basis of the 24/100/140 model, therefore, with its massive channel-section chassis frame, its I-section front axle suspended on half-

Left and below: The first of the overhead-camshaft engined six-cylinder supercharged cars designed by Dr Porsche was the 24/100/140. The body style of this 1924 tourer is by Saoutchik.
(Coys of Kensington Collection)

Right: The dashboard of the 1924 24/100/140 supercharged model.
(Coys of Kensington Collection)

Below right: The coachbuilt body shell of the 1924 24/100/140 model was as massive and substantial as the chassis which it graced.
(Coys of Kensington Collection)

*One of the first cars from the merged concerns –
a 1927 Model K Mercedes-Benz tourer.
(Coys of Kensington Collection)*

*The 1927 Model K tourer – showing that in
those days a luggage trunk was literally that,
and was entirely separate from the body itself.
(Coys of Kensington Collection)*

*In many ways the style of this 1927 Model K
was typical of the "vintage" period.
(Coys of Kensington Collection)*

This 1926 supercharged Mercedes-Benz tourer, has a modern registration number, but a "toast rack" body style and center-lock artillery-style wheels.
(Coys of Kensington Collection)

elliptic leaf springs, and with cantilever suspension of the back axle, a new series of Mercedes-Benz sports cars came to be developed and put on sale. Each seemed to be faster, more powerful (and more expensive) than the last, and it is true to say that Daimler-Benz always had more than half an eye on the competition potential of the cars.

The first obvious move was to make the car smaller and lighter, while at the same time making the engine larger and more powerful. The result, in 1926 (the year of the merger), was that the Type 24/110/160, or the K Type, was launched, where the K stood for "*Kurz*," which is German for "Short." This, incidentally, was still something of a relative term, for the new car's wheelbase was still a noble 11ft 2in (4.39m), and its fully equipped rolling chassis (without bodywork) still weighed in at nearly 3400lb (1542kg). The engine, however, had been enlarged to 381cu in (6246cc) [with a bore and stroke of 3.7×5.9in (94×150mm)]. Thus equipped, it was capable, for short periods with the supercharger engaged, of developing 160bhp.

What made this car immediately recognizable at the time, and legendary in the years which followed, was its exhaust system. At a time when almost every car had exhaust piping which was tucked discreetly under the chassis frame,

The 1926 "toast rack" model, before restoration by Coys.
(Coys of Kensington Collection)

This pre-merger Mercedes 24/100/140 Landaulette shows off the original three-pointed star variety of radiator badge, and the V radiator profile.
(Coys of Kensington Collection)

The 24/100/140 Landaulette of 1924 shows its very solid construction and a primitive type of (non-standard) direction indicator.
(Coys of Kensington Collection)

on the K-model and its successors the pipes were led proudly out through the side of the hood before being collected into a single tail pipe which then disappeared under the body sills. In most cases these pipes were built of flexible corrugated metal and highly plated or even polished. Because of the porting arrangements of the big six-cylinder engine, there were three such pipes of rather massive dimensions. In every way, therefore, this was a car for the proud and flamboyant owner — the styling spelt "power."

That, however, was just the start, for in 1927 the K-model was supplanted by the S-model, which was also rather ponderously known as the 26/120/180. Although a brief glance at that model name indicates that the engine was once again not only enlarged but boosted yet again, the main advance was in the

By 1927 the transformation of the Porsche-designed chassis into a genuine sporting machine was well underway. This was a 1927 "S" model tourer which has a very smart and practical radiator mesh screen.
(Coys of Kensington Collection)

This 1927 "S" model, seen here in North American surroundings, had a very spacious four-seater tourer body style.
(Coys of Kensington Collection)

The 1927 "S" model with one of the Sindelfingen-built tourer bodies for which the cars were so noted.
(Coys of Kensington Collection)

chassis design. The S—S for "Sporting"—benefited from an entirely new low chassis frame, in which the rearmost of the side-members was swept high over the line of the back axle, and in which half-elliptic leaf springs were underslung. There were additional cross-members to brace the frame, and the engine was moved back about 12in (30cm) in the frame itself. In spite of all this chassis development, however, the design still suffered from poor brakes, which were its weakest feature in the sports-car races for which it was designed—its acceleration and straight line speed were of the best, but its stopping power was not of the same standard. The S-model, incidentally, had much better brakes than the K-model, which must have been truly terrifying.

The S-model was not only fast but very flexible, for it could crawl along in top gear at a walking pace and (with supercharger engaged) it could also top the 100mph (160km/h) mark. To make this possible, the engine had once again been enlarged, to 414cu in (6789cc), due to the use of a 3.9in (98mm) cylinder bore and "wet" cylinder liners. The maximum (supercharged) power output was 180bhp, but factory-prepared racing models with higher compression ratios and special fuels turned out at least 220bhp. It was a car of this type which Otto Merz used to win the German Grand Prix of 1927. It was, of course, also very expensive—and exclusive—for only 142 cars were ever made.

More, however, was yet to come, as Porsche and Daimler-Benz indulged in what another author has described as "one-upmanship." In 1928 the SS-model appeared, with an official rating of 27/140/200, a 431cu in (7069cc) engine [and 4in (100mm cylinder bore)], and was also joined by the even more specialized SSK, rated as a 27/170/225. Here, for the first and last time, it will be noted that the British always had a different way of rating these cars. To the British, an S was a 36/220, while an SS was a 38/250, though at least they were happy to know an SSK by its official factory title. Incidentally,

When most owners of "vintage" cars saw a snout like this in their rear-view mirrors (if any) they usually moved over sharply. This was a supercharged 1927 "S" model.

although this was the last time that the engine was enlarged, it was certainly not the last time it was boosted. Power outputs in supercharged form rose to 300bhp (and marginally more in "sprint" racing form) in the early 1930s.

The SS—"Super Sports," a phrase which readily translates into German— remained the "standard" Daimler-Benz "supercar" until 1933, although only 111 cars were ever built in that time. It gave rise, however, to two further derivatives, the SSK which has already been mentioned, and the even more special and entirely impractical SSKL model. Both were intended purely for use in competitions, and both were the epitome, the ultimate expression, of what a truly "vintage" sports car should be.

The secret of their construction was spelled out in the letters "K" and "L." K, for "*Kurz*," meant that the chassis frames had been shortened yet again— this time from a wheelbase of 11ft 2in (4.39m) to one of 9ft 8in (3.75m)—while L, for "*Leight*" (or lightweight) meant that the car had been extensively lightened. Both cars, therefore, were considerably shorter than the definitive SS, and this was always perfectly obvious because most of the cars were fitted with very stark open two-seater sports bodies with exposed spare wheels, and because the style was dominated by the expanse of hood which covered the 433.2cu in (7.1-liter) supercharged engine. Only 33 SSKs were built between 1928 and 1932.

Dr Porsche left Stuttgart in 1928, and it was his successor Hans Nibel who directed the evolution of the extraordinary SSKL model. To Nibel, it seemed, there were only two ways in which the design could be improved without making radical changes: to increase the power output yet again, and to lighten the frame. There was no further "stretch" in the engine, so the power increase had to come from the use of the aptly named "elephant" blower, the largest of all the superchargers ever matched to the big engine. This, with very special attention to the camshaft and to the moving parts, allowed 300bhp to be available in extremis, though in fairness one should point out that it was as an unsupercharged 170bhp machine that the SSKL did most of its motoring. Officially, therefore, an SSKL was a 27/170/300 model.

The engine changes were not immediately obvious, unless anyone raising the hood knew all about the different sizes of superchargers used by Daimler-

Another name for the "S" model was (in British terms at least) the 36/220 Mercedes-Benz. This 1927 model had a modified body shell. (Coys of Kensington Collection)

The combination of a lowered chassis and a shorter wheelbase resulted in the SSK model of the late 1920s, which was so very successful on so many racing circuits.

Far left: The SSK's engine – what an impressive sight! The supercharger is the finned component at the front of the engine.

Center: The supercharger of the 38/250 SSK model is hidden. When it was engaged, the scream was quite unmistakable.

Left: The 1929 38/250 SSK model sports the obvious "trademarks" of three exhaust pipes through the hood panel and the big tail pipe, together with two spare wheels fixed to the abbreviated tail.

Above left: Not an SSK, which had a short wheelbase, but an SS, with a four-seater tourer body style. For racing – and this car was one such – a four-seater style was often compulsory. (Coys of Kensington Collection)

Center left: The heavy, ponderous, but very fast SS model of the 1929 period had a truly impressive racing record in "works" and in private hands. The brake drums virtually fill the space behind the wire spoke wheels. (Coys of Kensington Collection)

Below left: A detail of a racing 38/250 SS of 1929 shows the two different types of dampers controlling the front suspension. Note the stone starred "aero-screen" ahead of the passengers. (Coys of Kensington Collection)

1928 27/140/200 SS Sports Model [sometimes called 38/250 by British]

Engine: Six cylinders, in line, in four-bearing light-alloy combined block/crankcase. Bore and stroke, capacity: 3.94 × 5.9in, 431.4cu in (100 × 150mm, 7069cc). Detachable cast-iron cylinder head. Two overhead valves per cylinder, vertically mounted but staggered, and operated by fingers from single overhead camshaft. Two up-draft single-choke Mercedes-Benz carburetors with or without assistance from Roots-type supercharger, clutch-driven from nose of crankshaft. Maximum power: 200bhp (supercharged) and 140bhp (unsupercharged) at 3000rpm.

Transmission: Multi-dry-plate clutch and four-speed manual gearbox (without synchromesh), both in unit with front-mounted engine. Direct acting central gear-change. Propeller shaft enclosed in torque tube driving spiral-bevel "live" rear axle.

Chassis: Separate pressed-steel chassis frame with channel-section side-members and pressed or tubular cross-bracings. Forged front-axle beam. Front suspension by half-elliptic leaf springs. Rear suspension by half-elliptic leaf springs and torque tube location. Lever-arm hydraulic or friction-type dampers, to choice. Four-wheel, shaft-and-rod-operated drum brakes (some cars with vacuum servo assistance). Center-lock wire wheels. Tires: 6.50 × 20in. Choice of two-seater or four-seater sports/touring bodywork.

Dimensions: Wheelbase: 11ft 4in (3.45m). Front and rear tracks: 4ft 10in (1.47m). Overall length: 15ft 5in (4.70m). Unladen weight: 2800lb (1270kg).

Top: This front-end view of an SSK Mercedes-Benz does not allow the British rebodying details to be seen. However, . . . the same car, from a different viewpoint – center and above – shows the front fenders and the tail treatment which are more 1930s than late 1920s. (Coys of Kensington Collection)

Above mid center left: A 1928 Mercedes-Benz SS Cabriolet (above) . . . with some later (non-standard) touches to the body style (center left).

Below far left: Not one item of non-essential equipment appears on the front of this 1928 SS model.

Below left: Late-1920s Mercedes-Benz models were very fast and very well-equipped, but they tended to be slim and not over-endowed with passenger accommodation.

Below: A 1928 38/250 SS model, rebodied in the 1930s with more flowing fenders and a different tail. (Coys of Kensington Collection)

Benz, but the alterations applied to the chassis most certainly were. To reduce the car's weight as much as possible Nibel resorted to the age-old method of punching holes into every significant chassis member. This pared 250lb (113kg) off the weight but must have affected the frame's stiffness considerably and certainly had an adverse effect on the roadholding. Although the car was still a winner in the right hands, it could not possibly have pleased the orthodox engineering brains inside the company. It also begs the question that in S, SS and SSK form, the design must have been over-heavy all the time. The SSKL was so specialized and involved so much hand work that it was always purely a "works" competition car. Only a handful were ever built.

Even before the SSKL had been designed, however, Daimler-Benz had revealed its most magnificent touring car of all—a real flagship—the Grosser Type 770. Built in strictly limited numbers and intended for heads of state, dignitaries and businessmen of whom Daimler-Benz approved, the Grosser model was the most powerful touring car yet designed at Stuttgart, and was new from stem to stern. Central to the whole design was the brand new straight-eight, overhead-valve engine of 467.0cu in (7655cc), built on traditional "vintage" lines with a cast-iron block bolted to a separate light-alloy crankcase. As with the sporting models, there was a supercharger mounted at the front of the engine, which could be clutched in or out according to the driver's (or, in this case, more likely the chauffeur's) whim. It was built on a solid box-section chassis frame, with beam axle and half-elliptic spring suspension at front and rear, and always carried the most imposing sedan, limousine or drop-head body. Mechanically this chassis was distinguished by the fitment of a six-speed Maybach gearbox, power-assisted brakes (stopping it would have been almost impossible without assistance!), and an all-up weight without passengers of nearly 6000lb (2735kg). In seven years of production only 117 cars were built. Customers included ex-Kaiser Wilhelm II and Emperor Hirohito of Japan; the latter bought no fewer than seven examples and ran some of them until the mid-1960s.

Chronologically I must make a jump of several years, but in design terms the two cars were related—in 1937 the obsolete Grosser was dropped and replaced by a new Grosser model, which used the same engine and transmission (the engine now boosted to 155/230bhp instead of the 150/200 of the original model),

but a completely different tubular chassis frame, with a wheelbase of no less than 12ft 11in (5.01m), coil-spring independent suspension at front and a De Dion rear end. The frame was inspired by that of the Type W125 Grand Prix car, though naturally there were no common parts. It was even bigger, faster and more elephantine than ever—limousines were 20ft 6in (8.03m) long, and weighed more than 8000lb (3647kg), and that was without the optional armor-plating demanded by the Nazi party for some of the 88 cars built. Chauffeurs needed to be strong men, and brave men too, for a latter-day Grosser, when pressed, could approach top speeds of 110mph (177km/h). Naturally, fuel consumption was rarely better than five mpg. Quite a few of these cars survive, and when one changes hands it is almost to be expected that it is claimed once to have belonged to Hitler or Göring!

The sports cars and the limousines, however, were not the cars which Daimler-Benz needed, or used, to expand its operations. It was the conventional touring cars, at first with strictly mundane mechanical components but later with progressively more modern features, which allowed Daimler-Benz production to be expanded to nearly 28,000 cars a year in 1938. Immediately after the merger, Daimler-Benz set this process under way with two ranges which had been created by the design offices in 1925. Both had side-valve six-cylinder engines, solid chassis frames, flat radiators, and styling which must surely have been influenced by the fashions then prevailing in Detroit. The "Stuttgarts," built, as the name implies, in the Daimler factory

One of the first of the later type of Grosser Mercedes-Benz cars, this was built in 1938, complete with oval-tube chassis frame, De Dion rear suspension, and a 469.9cu in (7.7-liter) eight-cylinder engine. Such cars often weighed at least three tons. Like every car of its type this too is supposedly an "ex-Hitler car."

1938 Type 770 "Grosser" Model

Engine: Eight cylinders, in line, in cast-iron block, with separate nine-bearing light-alloy crankcase. Bore and stroke, capacity: 3.74×5.31in, 467cu in (95×135mm, 7655cc). Detachable cast-iron cylinder head. Two overhead valves per cylinder, operated by pushrods and rockers from single camshaft mounted in side of crankcase. Single up-draft Mercedes-Benz twin-choke carburetor with optionally engaged Roots-type super-charger, driven through friction clutch and gearing at nose of crankshaft and engaged by full movement of throttle pedal. Maximum power: 155bhp (unsupercharged) or 230bhp (supercharged) at 3500rpm.

Transmission: Single-dry-plate clutch and

five-speed synchromesh manual gearbox (no synchromesh on first gear), both in unit with front-mounted engine. Direct-acting central gearchange. Open propeller shaft to chassis-mounted spiral-bevel final-drive unit. Universally jointed drive shafts.

Chassis: Separate steel chassis frame made up of oval section tubes with tubular side-members, and tubular and pressed cross-bracings. Independent front suspension by coil springs and wishbones. De Dion rear suspension by coil springs, radius arms, and central tube location. Lever-arm hydraulic dampers. Worm-type steering. Four-wheel hydraulically operated drum brakes with servo assistance. Bolt-on 17in steel disk wheels. Tires: 8.25×17in. Open or closed ceremonial bodywork with four doors.

Dimensions: Wheelbase: 12ft 11.1in (3.94m). Front track: 5ft 4in, rear track: 5ft 6in (1.68m). Overall length: 20ft 6in (6.25m). Unladen weight (depending on coachwork, and on amount of armor-plating): 7600 to 8100lb (3447 to 3673kg).

in Stuttgart-Unterturkheim, had a small engine of 122.0cu in (2.0 liters) at first, which was enlarged to 158.7cu in (2.6 liters) in 1928, and were built until the early 1930s. The "Mannheims" were built at the Benz works in Mannheim, and had a different and rather larger engine. The 1926 model had a 189.2cu in (3.1-liter) engine size, but this was soon enlarged to 213.6cu in (3.5 liters), and eventually became a 225.8cu in (3.7-liter) unit in 1929. Although the "Stuttgarts" were never more than ordinary touring cars, the "Mannheims" eventually gave rise to the 370K (short wheelbase chassis) and 370S (sporting) derivatives. The 370S had a 223.4cu in (3663cc) engine developing 75bhp, and could reach a speed of about 75mph (120km/h)—creditable but, even by the standards of the day, not outstanding.

In addition to these quantity-production cars, there was also the larger, but still rather "vintage" and backward-looking, "Nurburg" range. Like the smaller cars, it also looked as if it had been influenced by Detroit, had a channel-section chassis frame, beam axle front and rear suspensions with half-elliptic leaf springs, a gearbox in unit with the engine, and central change. Its main selling point, however, was its straight-eight cylinder engine, a side-valve design sharing many components (including the same bore and stroke dimensions) with the 213.6cu in (3.5-liter) six-cylinder "Mannheim." At first it was sold as a 280.7cu in (4.6 liter), but in 1931 it was enlarged to 299.0cu in (4.9 liters) (and the same bore and stroke as the 370/370K/370S), and became known as the Nurburg 500. Although its coachwork was modernized during the 1930s, its basic chassis engineering was not, and it is rather remarkable to note that it was still in production in limited numbers at the end of the decade by which time about 3500 examples had been sold.

While all this consolidation and profit-making was going on, however, Hans Nibel and his team of engineers at Stuttgart were preparing to make a big technical leap forward out of the "vintage" era of conventional engineering into the future. Not only were they preparing to build the smallest-engined Mercedes-Benz car so far, but it would be the smallest and cheapest built by Daimler or Benz since the First World War, and it was to be equipped with all-independent suspension. With the world plunging inexorably into recession, the need for a small car was obvious (especially as the S/SS/SSK types were strictly for the rich and the self-indulgent), but to give that car an advanced suspension system was a brave move.

Cars with independent suspension had been built before, but the use of front-wheel *and* rear-wheel independent suspension in a series-production car was unique. Daimler-Benz first, and the rest of Continental Europe in due course, were well ahead of any other nation or continent in this respect.

The new car, announced in 1931, was the six-cylinder Type 170, the first of a whole new range and type of Mercedes-Benz models. In some ways it was only a half-way-house towards the cars which came later in the 1930s, for it still retained a box-section chassis frame and very understated styling. The real novelty, however, was hidden away in the shape of transverse leaf-spring independent front suspension, and independent rear suspension by means of a chassis-mounted differential, swinging half-axles and coil springs. Amid all this innovation, the disk wheels (most cars still used wire-spoke or artillery-style) went almost unnoticed. In its looks and in its performance [32bhp from the side-valve engine and a maximum speed of about 55mph (88km/h)] the Type 170 was unexciting, but in refinement and behavior it was a real advance.

The swing-axle rear suspension which was to become normal wear by all Mercedes-Benz production cars until the late 1960s, therefore, was born in this modest little 103.7cu in (1.7-liter) car. At the time, the merits or the draw-backs of using a system with so much potential camber change to the tires

One of the quantity-production Mercedes-Benz models of the mid-1930s, a six-cylinder Type 320 of 1937.
(Coys of Kensington Collection)

The flowing tail of the 1937 Type 320 Mercedes-Benz model was not at all common, and the enclosed spare wheel was a definite styling advance.
(Coys of Kensington Collection)

The frontal styling of the Type 320 was very "integrated" and shows signs of influence from Detroit.
(Coys of Kensington Collection)

were not questioned, nor were the effects very critical in such a limited-performance car. Later, as the cars became faster and more powerful and as tire characteristics changed, the system's limitations would be recognized. For years afterwards, however, and particularly in the 1960s, it became a matter of pride that Daimler-Benz was not going to admit to an error in choosing this as one of its "trademarks" and the final generations of swing-axle suspension went to all lengths to give acceptable roadholding.

It is important, however, to realize that the Type 170 also ushered in the use of hydraulic brakes, central chassis lubrication and other details which would be used more and more often in the Daimler-Benz range of the future. Once launched, the Type 170 was soon joined by other derivatives such as the Type 200 of 1932 which was technically the same type of car, but with a 122.0cu in (2.0-liter) six-cylinder engine and 40bhp. Nearly 14,000 Type 170s were built in five years, and the Type 200 was even more popular.

A year later the Type 290 was introduced, and things began to get thoroughly confusing. Not only was yet another type and size of side-valve six-cylinder engine used, but the independent front suspension was of another type, incorporating a transverse leaf spring and coil springs compressed by an extension of the top wishbones. The car's power output was 68bhp, and its top speed was about 70mph (113km/h).

By 1936 the 200 had grown up into the Type 230 with a 136.0cu in (2229cc) engine, while the 290 had evolved into the Type 320 in which the engine had been enlarged to 195.7cu in (3208cc), and they had been equipped with all-synchromesh gearboxes. In the meantime, Daimler-Benz engineers and sales staff had noted that an opportunity was present to sell cars even smaller than the Type 170 and Type 200 models. To fill this gap they made their most ambitious move so far (and, in the eyes of some critics, their first big mistake) — they designed another brand new chassis, this time fitted with a rear engine.

The rear-engined concept had been circulating in Germany for some time (Dr Porsche was already working on prototypes for firms like Zundapp), and was thought to be the best way to maximize the passenger accommodation inside a small car. The Daimler-Benz solution was to design a frame with a sturdy tubular backbone, one which supported its front suspension (independent, by transverse leaf spring) on simple cross-members, and which incorporated a tuning-fork shape of pressed steel extension which embraced and supported the engine which was mounted behind the line of the rear wheels. The gearbox was ahead of that line, and the gear linkage led forward alongside the tube. Rack and pinion steering was a feature, as was the mounting of the cooling radiator above the swing-axle rear suspension. Four-cylinder engines were used, the first being a 79.3cu in (1.3-liter) side-valve unit which was no more and no less than two-thirds of the Type 200 six-cylinder unit.

The trouble with the Type 130H (H meant *heck* or rear) was that it was underpowered with only 26bhp, rather heavy, and its handling was very strange. Daimler-Benz, like Porsche and later VW, discovered that the combination of swing-axle rear suspension and a rearward bias to the weight distribution of the car can have daunting effects on stability. Daimler-Benz, as always, however, tried hard to make it work, and sold nearly 10,000 of these stubby VW-like touring cars. They also developed a more attractive sports-car version of the chassis, known as the 150H, which had a 91.5cu in (1.5-liter) 55bhp engine with an overhead-camshaft layout mounted ahead of the line of the rear wheels, and therefore surely qualified as the first modern mid-engined car ever to be put on sale. Very few were made.

One last attempt was made to sell rear-engined cars to the public, with the Type 170H of 1935, which used an enlarged 103.5cu in (1697cc) side-valve

Left above: Built for high speed on the new German autobahns was this "Autobahn Kurier" Type 500K, which had a 305.1cu in (5.0 liter) eight-cylinder engine and independent front suspension.

Left center: Rearward vision from the Type 500K was extremely limited, but the aerodynamics looked good.

Left below: The 1934 500K with its smooth coupe body style was good for around 100mph (160km/h), and on the new German high-speed roads such speeds were often exercised.

Right above: Tom Barrett's impressive and, in a way, very Teutonic 500K Cabriolet, built in 1935.

Right center: The 1934 500K Cabriolet was the actual and the spiritual successor to the Porsche-designed cars of the 1920s.

Right below: This shapely 500K Cabriolet body was built by Daimler-Benz in the Sindelfingen body construction factory.

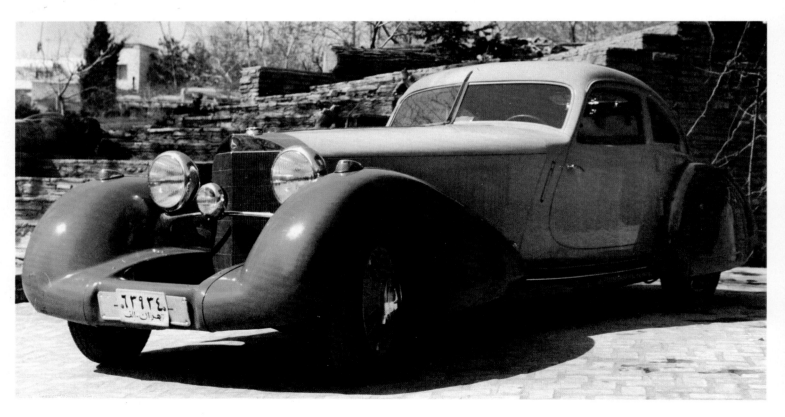

The sartorial elegance of the 1935 500K.

version of the 130H's engine and had 38bhp which resulted in more reasonable performance. The public, however, was far more interested in the more conventional-looking Stuttgart products, and the last of these interesting, but relatively unsuccessful, rear-engined cars were built in 1938.

In the meantime, Daimler-Benz had astonished the world in 1936 by putting the first-ever series-production diesel-powered car on sale. The engineers had intended to market a large 231.9cu in (3.8-liter) diesel engine in a Mannheim type of chassis in the early 1930s, but found that far too much vibration was present and abandoned the experiment. Their second thoughts—very successful and historic ones—were to develop a 158.7cu in (2.6-liter) four-cylinder diesel from the same basic design, and to install it in a Type 230 chassis. This worked much better and was duly put on sale in 1936. Although the power output was limited to 45bhp at 3000rpm, the car could reach 60mph (97km/h) even with a heavy body, and it soon found a market not only among taxi operators, but among private buyers looking for cars with long-life potential. Note, however, that this engine was not produced after the Second World War, as a new and smaller diesel unit was developed for that period.

The culmination of Daimler-Benz series-production passenger-car design-thinking came in 1935 and 1936, when a new range of tubular chassis began to be introduced. Not only were tubes used instead of box-section pressed members, but they were laid out in the form of a backbone down the center of the car. The by-now-traditional Daimler-Benz independent suspensions were also specified—with transverse leaf springs at the front and coil springs and swing axles at the rear.

At the same time as the last of the rear-engined models, the 170H, was being shown, the front-engined 170V made its appearance, and was immediately seen to be a very advanced but more conventional car. Instead of the box-section frame of the superseded 170 and 200 models, the 170V had a tubular backbone frame, and a front-mounted 103.7cu in (1.7-liter) side-valve four-cylinder engine exactly like that used in the rear-engined 170H. The styling of the new car was restrained, but unmistakeably Daimler-Benz, and even though it was not at all forward-looking, it would still be a part of the Stuttgart and Sindelfingen scene in the early 1950s. It was available with several different Sindelfingen-built separate bodies, including delivery vehicles and ambulances, and more than 90,000 examples were built before production was suspended at the end of 1942. In the same year the 230 was launched with the same chassis but with the 140.3cu in (2.3-liter) version of the familiar side-valve six-cylinder engine and with remarkably similar styling. Lastly, in 1937, the Type 320 appeared, with the 195.3cu in (3.2-liter) six-cylinder engine, but still with the old type of box-section frame.

Daimler-Benz management was no doubt philosophical about the way in which the front-engined 170V speedily elbowed aside the rear-engined 170H. Although the rear-engined car was kept, somewhat haltingly, in production until the end of the decade, it could surely not have been because it was profitable. In 1936, when both cars were on sale together for the first time, 12,683 170Vs were built, against a mere 1101 rear-engined 170Hs. Overall in five years, 1507 170Hs were built, which compared very badly with 65,439 170Vs. However, the 170V was not only valuable for what it did in the 1930s, but for the way it so ably filled the gap between the end of World War Two and the arrival of the first true postwar design. In more ways than one, perhaps, the 170V was the car which ensured the ultimate survival of Daimler-Benz AG.

One range of models has remained deliberately unsurveyed until the end of this chapter because they were the most glamorous of all 1930s Daimler-Benz products. Starting from the release of the Type 380 Sports tourer of 1933 and

Right: The final flowering of the 370K of 1931 was the 540K of 1936, which had a 329.5cu in (5.4-liter) eight-cylinder engine with optionally operated supercharger. Most of the available bodies, like this Cabriolet, were by Daimler-Benz.

Right below: The 540Ks could get up to 100mph (160km/h), at which speed they devoured gasoline at least as fast as any latter-day Detroit juggernaut. They were very exclusive, and very impressive too.

1936 Type 540K sports-tourer

Engine: Eight cylinders, in line, in nine-bearing cast-iron cylinder block/crankcase. Bore and stroke, capacity: 3.46×4.37in, 329.6cu in (88×111mm, 5401cc). Detachable cast-iron cylinder head. Two overhead valves per cylinder, operated by pushrods and rockers from single camshaft mounted in side of cylinder block. Single up-draft Mercedes-Benz carburetor, with optionally engaged Roots-type supercharger, driven through friction clutch and gearing from nose of crankshaft, and engaged by full movement of throttle pedal. Maximum power: 115bhp (unsupercharged) or 180bhp (supercharged) at 3600rpm.

Transmission: Single-dry-plate clutch and four-speed synchromesh manual gearbox (no synchromesh on first gear), both in unit with front-mounted engine. Direct-acting central gearchange. Open propeller shaft to chassis-mounted spiral-bevel final drive. Universally jointed drive shafts enclosed in swinging half axles.

Chassis: Separate pressed-steel box-section chassis frame, with box-section cross-bracing. Automatic chassis lubrication. Independent front suspension by coil springs and wishbones. Independent rear suspension by swing axles and double coil springs (one in front, one behind, the half-shaft line). Lever-arm hydraulic dampers. Worm-type steering. Four-wheel hydraulically operated drum brakes, with Bosch vacuum servo assistance. Bolt-on 17in wire wheels. Tires: 7.00×17in. Variety of coachwork—cabriolet, sports, coupe, and others.

Dimensions: Wheelbase: 10ft 9.5in (3.29m). Front track: 4ft 11.5in (1.51m), rear track: 4ft 11in (1.50m). Overall length: 17ft 2.5in (5.25m). Unladen weight (depending on coachwork): (approx) 5000lb (2268kg).

culminating in the magnificent 540K models of the late 1930s, it was a design which typified everything which was grand, assertive, pompous and spectacular about Germany under the influence of Adolf Hitler. Although it was not a direct mechanical relation of the S/SS/SSK models, this family was certainly its spiritual descendant, for although the Type 770 Grosser was the biggest and most costly, the cars now remembered as 540Ks were the fastest.

The Type 380 was launched in 1933 as a 380K sports model and was one of the last projects masterminded by Hans Nibel before he died in 1934. As revealed at the Paris Show, it had a low box-section chassis frame with coil spring and wishbone front suspension and the usual type of Mercedes-Benz swing-axle rear suspension, also controlled by coil springs. The real interest, however, was shown in the 233.1cu in (3822cc) engine, which was a straight-eight with single overhead camshaft, a bore and stroke of 3.1×3.9in (78×100mm), and was not at all connected with any other Daimler-Benz power

Below: A 1934 500K Cabriolet with rakish lines.
(Coys of Kensington Collection)

Bottom: This 1934 500K model combines up-to-date lines and all the comforts of a well-engineered Cabriolet body with the exposed exhaust pipes made famous on Mercedes-Benz models in the 1920s.
(Coys of Kensington Collection)

unit. As with the earlier large 433.2cu in (7.1-liter) and 469.9cu in (7.7-liter) Daimler-Benz engines, this was fitted with a supercharger, whose operation could be clutched into or out of engagement by the final depression of the accelerator pedal. Without the supercharger in use, it was rated at 90bhp, but with supercharger the figure rose to 120bhp.

This was no better than the outputs claimed by firms like Invicta and Lagonda for their 274.6cu in (4.5-liter) Meadows-engined cars, and it seemed to be true that the 380K could be outpaced by several of the best and latest French Grand Tourers. In addition, it was a much more supple car than the SSK which it replaced, and the word soon got around that it was not a proper sports car at all. Although this criticism was not all justified, it was quite true that the 380K was somewhat overweight, so in 1934 it was replaced after a very short run by the 500K, which had an enlarged engine of 306.1cu in (5018cc) [with a bore and stroke of 3.4 × 4.3in (86 × 108mm)], and a maximum

One of the famous SSK chassis with a post-World War II body style by Saoutchik. (Coys of Kensington Collection)

Left: This eight-cylinder 540K chassis is hidden by a rather unusual tourer body style. (Coys of Kensington Collection)

Center: Under that svelte and Teutonic exterior is an eight-cylinder supercharged engine of the 500K/540K type. The spare wheel looks perilously close to the hot external exhaust pipe. (Coys of Kensington Collection)

Below: By the mid-1930s even an eight-cylinder supercharged Mercedes-Benz Cabriolet had an enclosed trunk compartment. (Coys of Kensington Collection)

An evocative example of the supercharged 540K model, dating from 1936. (Coys of Kensington Collection)

output *mit kompressor* of 160bhp. With similarly styled bodies, many having sweeping lines by the Daimler-Benz stylists at Sindelfingen but some with coachbuilt shells, a 500K was capable of 100mph (160km/h), subject to the usual caveat that the supercharger should only be used for very limited periods.

But it was not merely the performance or the handling of these cars which was so devastatingly attractive—it was the styling. Sindelfingen produced several different versions of which the two seat roadster was undoubtedly the most outstanding. The combination of arrogant "V"-shaped radiator, the proudly displayed three-pointed star, the steeply raked windshield, the smoothly swept front and rear fenders, the long hood and the swept and chiseled rear deck, all added up to the sort of car which finds its way into advertisements, fantasies, and the book of legends.

Daimler-Benz, however, was not satisfied, for in 1936 the company converted the 500K into the 540K with a capacity of 329.5cu in (5401cc) [bore and stroke of 3.5×4.4in (88×111mm)], and a supercharged output of no less than 180bhp. This was the ultimate production Mercedes-Benz of the 1930s, as it could easily beat 105mph (169km/h)—which was considered phenomenal for a road car of the day—even if the fuel consumption was usually worse than ten miles per gallon.

Over 700 of the 500Ks and 540Ks were built between 1934 and 1939, but even they might have been overshadowed by the 580K of 1939, if it had ever gone into production. As it was, only about a dozen cars were built before the war intervened, and few people ever sampled the delights of the five-speed gearbox, and the promise of quite unheard-of top speeds.

Without any doubt, however, the 540K was the car by which many of us will always remember the "original" Daimler-Benz concern. The word "original" is used because the company which disappeared in the holocaust of the 1939–1945 War was very different from that rebuilt so painstakingly and so successfully in the 1940s and 1950s.

The merger of Daimler with Benz made little difference to either company's enthusiasm for motor racing. Both had been successful in the past, and both were determined to be successful, in partnership, in the future.

5. THREE-POINTED STAR IN MOTORSPORT

It is generally agreed that the great motor-racing era of the 1920s and 1930s was dominated by supercharged cars, but far too many people credit the wrong firm with pioneering the idea. While it is true that Chadwick (in the USA) produced the world's first "blown" racing car in 1908 and Fiat the first supercharged Grand Prix car in 1923, Europe's first supercharged racing *and* road cars were built by Mercedes in 1922. Fiat, however, did not remain in motor racing long, and did not reap the benefits of its early experience. On the other hand, Mercedes and later Mercedes-Benz built up so much expertise with "blown" engines that each and every one of their successful competition cars up until 1939 was fitted with a supercharged engine.

It was undoubtedly the development pressures of the First World War, and particularly those from aero-engine customers, which first led Daimler to develop supercharged engines. Without a doubt it was the firm's aero-engine experience, which dated from 1915, which led it to adapt the principle to motorcar engines for the 1920s. The fact, therefore, that a new principle was evolved to stop airplane engines "running out of breath" as they climbed higher into the sky was directly responsible for the enormous progress made by Daimler-Benz in the 1920s and 1930s.

The theory of supercharging is easily explained but it is by no means as easy to develop and refine. Normally aspirated engines take in fuel-air mixture to their cylinders by suction, and if the air supply is restricted or is of reduced density, then the engine power falls away. If, on the other hand, an engine-driven pump can be arranged to force air into the cylinders at an increased pressure, then more power will be produced. It takes power to drive the pump, but a great deal more than this is produced in the process. Within the limits of metallurgical and fuel technology, this is almost a classic case of "power for free"; it is one of the few authentic cases known to man where dragging oneself up by one's own bootstraps really works.

It was also a perfect way of cheating motorsport's legislators — by effectively increasing the swept volume of engine being built for a restricted capacity formula. Mercedes and Fiat both took great advantage of this in the early days, and it was not until 1938 that a Grand Prix formula was devised which differentiated between the maximum allowable size of supercharged and unsupercharged engines. Once the enormous advantages were widely understood, however, almost every manufacturer adopted supercharging. As Laurence Pomeroy so succinctly stated in his famous book about Grand Prix racing: "The Italian Grand Prix of 1923 was the first international race to be won by a supercharged car and from then until 1939 only one event of this status was won without a blower, except on those occasions when supercharging had been proscribed by the regulations . . ."

Therefore, although Mercedes was first in the field with a supercharged car — the company was actually selling road cars before it started to race — it was not the first to benefit by so doing. The firm did, however, invent a method of operation which was, at the time, unique, and one which gave the driver the option of having a supercharged car or not.

The process started with two cars introduced at the Berlin Motor Show of 1921 — the 6/25/40 and 10/40/65 models, which had 91.5cu in (1.5-liter) and 158.7cu in (2.6-liter) engines respectively. As the model-naming system used was to persist on Mercedes and Mercedes-Benz cars for some years, it should be explained: for example, in the case of the 10/40/65, the "10" referred to a fiscal horsepower rating, the "40" to the maximum power produced by the engine without the use of the supercharger, and the "65" referred to the maximum power produced with the supercharger in operation.

Previous page: The nose and front suspension of that most powerful of all Mercedes-Benz racing cars, the W125 of 1937.

On these original cars as on every future supercharged Mercedes and Mercedes-Benz road car (though not on all the special competition cars), the supercharger, which was a twin-rotor Roots type, was mounted at the front of the engine. It was only brought into operation by an extension of the throttle linkage, which operated a multi-disk clutch at the nose of the crankshaft; this only happened when the driver pressed the accelerator pedal to the floorboards, when an extra pressure was felt. However, because the engines were built and stressed principally for unsupercharged use, operation of the "optional" Mercedes supercharging was always hedged around with dire instructions from the manufacturers and was a decidedly temporary business. To use supercharging all the time on the road cars was considered certain to result in a destroyed engine, and to use it for more than about a minute at a time was definitely considered adventurous. Incidentally, the 10/40/65 used a four-cylinder single-overhead-camshaft engine built on very much the same lines as the 1914 Grand Prix engine and to which supercharging was applied during development, whereas the 6/25/40 was the first Mercedes engine to be designed from the outset to include supercharging.

The scene was now set for the return of Mercedes to top-level motor racing, and after Sailer's encouraging run in the 1921 Targa Florio in an unsupercharged 28/95, it was decided to enter not only a supercharged 28/95 for the

Max Sailer at the wheel of his victorious 28/95 Mercedes sports car in the 1921 Coppa Florio, run in conjunction with the Targa Florio.

1922 race, but a supercharged 91.5cu in (1.5-liter) car (using a heavily modified 6/25/40 engine—so modified, in fact, that it was the first-ever Mercedes
to have a twin-overhead-camshaft cylinder head) and no fewer than three of
the superlative 1914 Grand Prix cars, converted with fenders and windshields
to look like sports cars! It was Count Masetti, driving one of the converted
Grand Prix cars which was now his own property, who won the Targa Florio
outright from a couple of fast Ballots, with Max Sailer finishing sixth in the
outdated and outpaced supercharged 28/95 model.

Although Mercedes could now have re-entered Grand Prix racing, they chose
instead to mount an assault on the United States. With an aggressive export
campaign in mind for their road cars, it was decided to enter a team of cars for
the 1923 Indianapolis 500 race where, co-incidentally, the latest 122.0cu in
(2.0-liter) Grand Prix formula had just been adopted. It must have crossed the
mind of the engineers at Stuttgart that they might be able to use these cars in
Grand Prix racing as well, before they were outpaced.

The 1923 Mercedes Indianapolis 500 race car was the last to be designed
under the direction of Paul Daimler, who was to move on, early in 1923, to
become technical director of Horch, and it was one of the first of a whole series
of magnificent racing engines to be evolved at Stuttgart by Otto Schilling.
Like the 1922 Targa Florio engine, it had a twin-overhead-camshaft cylinder
head, and used welded-up (aero-engine style) construction. Like all racing
engines of the day, it was considerably "undersquare" (which is to say that it
had a cylinder bore of 2.8in (70mm), a stroke of 5.1in (129mm), and a capacity
from its four-cylinder layout of 121.3cu in (1989cc). The unit was supercharged
in what had already become known as the "usual" Mercedes method. The
chassis layout was strictly conventional by Mercedes standards, and like all
such cars from Stuttgart it was equipped with an exhaust system whose
manifold pipes sprouted directly out of the side of the hood panel. It was
something of a Mercedes trademark which would persist until the 1930s.

The Indianapolis expedition was something of a disaster for Mercedes for
these were not easy cars to drive. Lautenschlager's car crashed and the best
Max Sailer could do was to finish in eighth place while Werner took eleventh
place. The 120bhp engines, however, had proved themselves to be very
reliable, if none too flexible, and the cars were only just competitive among
other 122.0cu in (2.0-liter) machines. In the meantime, however, an event of
great importance had occurred at Stuttgart. The technical responsibilities laid
down by Paul Daimler had been assumed by Dr Ferdinand Porsche, who had
moved in from Austro-Daimler in Austria. Although Porsche arrived too late
to influence the fortunes of the Indianapolis 500 cars, he was quite determined
to make great changes in the future.

Professor Dr Ferdinand Porsche, to give him his full title, was born in the
backwoods of Bohemia in 1875, the son of a plumber. He found no time to take
a university degree course, but became fascinated by electricity and designed
his first car, the electrically powered Lohner-Porsche, in 1900. In 1906 he
joined Austro-Daimler, became its technical chief after Paul Daimler moved
back to Daimler at Stuttgart, and thus followed him from one job to the next,
17 years later.

At Stuttgart Porsche's first job was to improve the 1923 Indianapolis design,
which he did with a vengeance. Not only did the cars dominate the 1924 San
Sebastian Grand Prix for the first 165 miles (265km) (after which Count Masetti
crashed the leading car), but in sports-car guise they also won the 1924 Targa
Florio with Werner driving. It is not without significance that the third driver
in the Targa Florio team, who finished in 15th place, was a 33-year old man
named Alfred Neubauer. . . .

Rudi Caracciola, the most famous and successful of all Mercedes-Benz racing drivers in the interwar period.

The Solitude-Rennen of May 1924 with Otto Merz (Car No 15) and Carl Sailer (No 14) in four-cylinder supercharged 122.0cu in (2.0-liter) models (the Targa Florio models) at the start line.

While all this was going on, however, Porsche was heavily involved in another completely new car—the first eight-cylinder Grand Prix car ever to carry the badge of the three-pointed star. This car, although elegantly detailed and undoubtedly very powerful (it had 170bhp—considerably more than the four-cylinder car of a year earlier), was always considered tricky to handle. A team of four cars was entered for the Italian Grand Prix at Monza in October 1924 (the race should have been held in September but so many teams, including Mercedes, struck trouble in practice that the race was postponed for six weeks—consider the likelihood of that happening today!), but although Count Masetti was in second place after the first lap, the challenge soon faded, and tragedy intervened when Count Louis Zborowski crashed his car and was killed. The son, like the father, had perished when racing for Mercedes. After that, there was no heart left for a battle with the Alfa Romeo P2s, and the other two Mercedes "eights" were flagged off by Max Sailer, who was now acting as team manager rather than driver.

Many things, it seemed, were wrong with the original design (but could surely have been made good if development had been carried forward). The suspension was rock hard, the roadholding suspect and there was virtually no low-speed torque, a problem compounded by the use of only three forward gears. In one way, however, it was something of a "prototype" for future Mercedes-Benz racing cars. It was the first car from Stuttgart to have permanent instead of "clutched" supercharging.

Two years later, immediately after the merger between Daimler and Benz, a couple of much-modified "eights" with four-seater "sports-car" bodies were entered for the first-ever German Grand Prix which was held on the Avus track. One car crashed badly, but Rudolph Caracciola in his first "works" drive

Otto Merz at the wheel of the 122.0cu in (2.0 liter) "Targa Florio" type of Mercedes racing car.

for Daimler-Benz steered the other car to victory.

For Ferdinand Porsche, however, this exquisite but only partly developed Grand Prix car was a mere diversion, and an expensive one at that. Apart from its possible value as a marketing and advertising tool, it was of no commercial significance. However, the other cars on which the brilliant Austrian had been working ever since his arrival in April 1923 undoubtedly were. For Porsche's principal task at Stuttgart in those first few months was to oversee the design of two new supercharged six-cylinder cars which owed nothing to previous designs, and were vital to the company's future.

The two cars were of very similar mechanical design, though the 15/70/100 model had a 239.1cu in (3920cc) engine, and the 24/100/140 had a rather larger 380.8cu in (6242cc) engine. It was the engines themselves and the characteristic screaming noises emitted by the superchargers when in use which made the cars so distinctive for the chassis design was strictly conventional. The big car, indeed, was so big [its wheelbase in the original version was no less than 12ft 3.5in (4.82m)] and heavy that it did not look like the basis of a good competition car. The 24/100/140, incidentally, was an up-market replacement for the old 28/95, and shared that car's cylinder dimensions of 3.7×5.9in (94×150mm). Also like the 28/95 and the successful Targa Florio cars of 1924, the year in which they made their appearance, the cars proudly wore an aggressive "V"-shaped radiator.

From 1925 to 1933 derivatives of the larger Porsche design upheld the

Otto Merz in a unique type of eight-cylinder Mercedes racing car at Solitude, in 1926.

Mercedes and Mercedes-Benz names on the race tracks of the world, though Dr Porsche, himself, left Mercedes-Benz in 1928, following violent disagreements over future policy, and made his way to Steyr. It was not until the early 1930s, when his newly constituted design bureau was commissioned to provide a brand-new Grand Prix car for the use of Auto-Union that he once again came into indirect contact with Daimler-Benz. To list all the successes gained by K, S, SS, SSK and SSKL derivatives would fill a complete book, but they can be summarized by mentioning the Mille Miglia, the Tourist Trophy, the German Grand Prix, the Irish Grand Prix, the Eifelrennen, the Argentine Grand Prix and the 24 Hours of Spa. The "star" of the team was undoubtedly Rudolph Caracciola, a world-class driver by any standards but apparently quite unbeatable in the rain. He was a man who was to remain faithful to Daimler-Benz for the rest of his racing life.

In 1926 the short-chassis K-model was ready, and Alfred Neubauer became Daimler-Benz's team manager for the first time. Although a team of Ks won its class in the San Sebastian 12-hour race, the cars were not the fastest in the race, and for 1927 the low-chassis S-model was used instead. Its racing debut at the new Nurburgring track was sensational, for Caracciola won the first event ever held there, and a month later the S-models of Merz, Werner and Walb took the first three places in the German Grand Prix on the same circuit.

In 1928 the larger-engined and more powerful SS made its debut in the German Grand Prix and dominated the race with Caracciola winning from

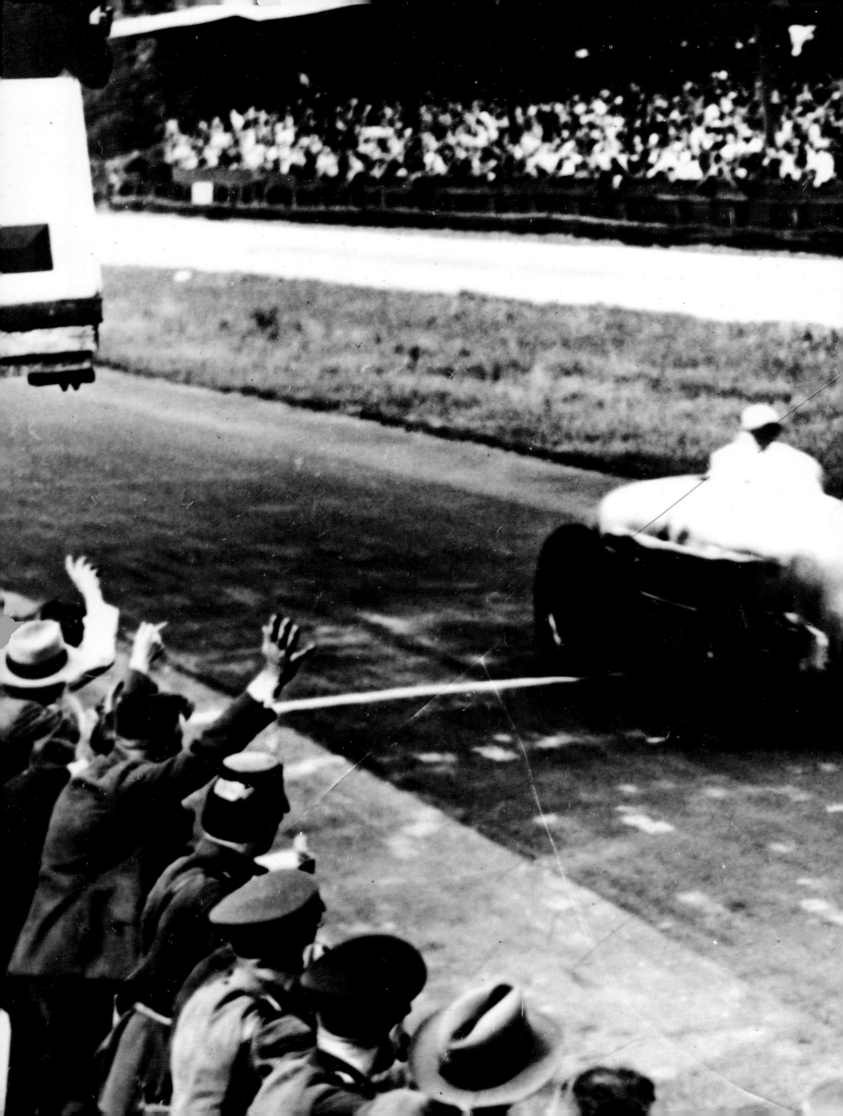

Manfred von Brauchitsch in the specially streamlined SSKL model of 1932, which won the race for over 91.5cu in (1500cc) cars at the Avus track in May of that year. The shape was an ancestor of the later "Silver Arrow" Grand Prix cars.

Top: The short-chassis SSK sports model was used for racing. Its engine produced 170hp without supercharger or a maximum of 220hp with the supercharger engaged. It was also known as the 38/250 model.

Above: A fine "S" type model with its six-cylinder supercharged engine, which produced a maximum of 120hp (or 180hp with the supercharger engaged).

Merz and Werner. The even-shorter chassised SSK two-seater also appeared in 1928, but made its first headlines in 1929 when Caracciola drove one into third place in the Monaco Grand Prix (which was held under "Formula Libre" rules that year), after leading for many miles. Later in the year Caracciola won a wet Tourist Trophy race in Northern Ireland in an SS model.

The following year was very eventful for Daimler-Benz, for Caracciola could only finish sixth in his first attempt at winning the Mille Miglia (in an SSK), blew up at Le Mans after being harried unmercifully by the entire Bentley team, won the Irish Grand Prix on handicap, and also became European Mountain Champion. The versatile German would undoubtedly have been a strong contender for victory in the 1930 TT, but his SS was not allowed to start because it was fitted with a larger than standard "elephant" blower.

By this time even the splendid SSK was becoming outclassed, and for 1931 the drastically lightened and even more powerful SSKL model, never sold to the public, was developed. With it Caracciola had an incredibly successful year, which began with an epic drive to victory in the Mille Miglia (during which he broke the course record), and continued with wins at Avus, the Nurburgring (twice), the Eifelrennen, and the German Grand Prix. In 1932

Rudi Caracciola (Mercedes-Benz SSK) on his way to victory in the Avus-Rennen of 1931. He was supreme in this type of car.

and 1933 because of the economic depression, there was very little Daimler-Benz racing activity, though Manfred von Brauchitsch drove a specially streamlined SSKL to victory in the large-car race at the Avus track in 1932, the car having a style which must surely have had an effect on the Mercedes-Benz racing cars which were to follow it.

Two vital events then followed which also molded the shape and scope of Daimler-Benz's sporting activities for the rest of the 1930s. In October 1932 motorsport's governing body announced a new Grand Prix formula to come into effect in January 1934, and in January 1933 Adolf Hitler became Chancellor of Germany. On the one hand, Daimler-Benz was attracted by the idea of an enforceable formula which allowed constructors a free hand if their cars weighed no more than 1653lb (750kg) without tires and fluids, and, on the other, the company was pleased to find that the German Transport Ministry was prepared to pay an annual subsidy and event-by-event prize moneys to German makers of Grand Prix cars. The decision to re-enter Grand Prix racing was made in March 1933, and the cars were expected to be ready early the following year. Hans Nibel was to be in charge overall, and the experimental department which was to build the cars was run by Fritz Nallinger.

The new Grand Prix Mercedes-Benz car was known as the Type W25, and got down to the 1653lb weight limit by a liberal use of light-alloys. Compared with the established (one almost said "traditional") Grand Prix cars from Bugatti and Alfa Romeo, the W25 was radical, startling, and made a great impression on anyone who saw it for the first time. Not only was it very different from the Alfas and the Bugattis, but it was also quite unlike the SSKLs.

Whereas the Alfa/Bugatti tradition was to have their engines mounted in channel-section chassis frames with ultra-hard non-independent leaf-spring suspensions, all clothed in a rigidly upright and angular body shell, Nibel's W25 had a box-section frame, low lines, all-independent suspension, and an engine with undoubted potential. Neither was it unnecessarily complex and advanced, for even while work was going ahead at Stuttgart it became known that Dr Porsche had also produced a really startling design for Auto-Union, which not only had most of the advances to be found in the W25 but a tubular frame and a V16 cylinder engine mounted behind the driver.

The heart of the W25, however, was the straight-eight cylinder, twin-overhead-camshaft engine, built in the usual Daimler-Benz manner from a mixture of light alloy castings and light steel water jackets. In three years it was enlarged from 205.0cu in (3360cc) [3.1 × 3.5in (78 × 88mm) bore and stroke] to 345.3cu in (5660cc) [3.7 × 4.0in (94 × 102mm)], during which period the power was pushed up from about 350bhp at 5800rpm to an occasional 646bhp at the same engine speed.

At first, in truth, the independent front suspension with stiff coil springs hidden inside a cross-member was far too stiff, and the swing-axle rear suspension was always something of a hazard to predictable roadholding, but the car was undoubtedly very fast. For the next four seasons Mercedes-Benz and Auto-Union cars swept the traditional French and Italian cars aside in a display of Teutonic engineering, efficiency, and dedication, which set entirely new standards in Grand Prix racing. For all that, however, the cars were still too heavy when weighed—by just two pounds—and as a desperate measure Neubauer ordered that every atom of the white paint should be sanded off the bodywork! This was done, the weight reduction was sufficient, and overnight the cars achieved their nickname of *Silberfeile*, or Silver Arrows, for this was the color and style of their light-alloy body skins.

The development, success—and occasional failure—of these eight-cylinder cars is known so well that no more than a summary is needed here of their fortunes. Throughout their life the cars were entered only for World Championship Grands Prix, for the occasional race where a political or marketing

Left: Caracciola's W25 Mercedes-Benz Grand Prix in the 1935 Barcelona Grand Prix, where he finished second to Fagioli in a sister car.

Above: The W25 models at the start line of the 1935 Monaco Grand Prix, won by Fagioli.

presence was required, or for some of the long-distance European hill climbs.

Cars were on test at Monza by March 1934, though it was the rival Auto-Union which raced first. On its maiden racing appearance, however, the W25 won the 214-mile (344km) (non-Championship) Eifel race with Manfred von Brauchitsch driving. A month later in the French Grand Prix, teething troubles slowed them down, and Fagioli's car was second to Stuck's Auto-Union. Fagioli went on to win the Italian Coppa Acerbo, the Italian Grand Prix (sharing the driving with Caracciola) and the Spanish Grand Prix, with another second in the Czech Grand Prix.

In 1935 the W25s, now with 400bhp 244cu in (4.0-liter) "eights," and aided by the development of the ZF limited-slip differentials, won five out of seven Grands Prix, four other events, and Caracciola (who had still been recovering in 1934 from his 1933 Monaco crash in which his thigh was badly broken) became European Champion. In 1936, however, Daimler-Benz developed the short-

Left: The streamlined version of a 1937 W125 Grand Prix car, as driven to victory at the Avus circuit by Hermann Lang in May 1937, at the shattering average speed of 163.6mph (261.7km/h).

Right: Hermann Lang (goggles on head) and Alfred Neubauer (on his left) at the finish of the Avus races of May 1937. The delighted executive in the hat is Max Sailer.

Below: At the Avus race in May 1937, Caracciola's car (No 35) leads one of the mid-engined Auto-Union models on the famous steep paved banking. On this occasion Caracciola's car failed to finish.

chassis W25/1936, which was distinguished by the fitment of De Dion rear suspension, and by the fact that (in racing historian Karl Ludvigsen's words) "it was a crushing failure." That was the year in which no amount of power— 450bhp with 286.8cu in (4.7-liter) engines—could make up for the poor road-holding and response. Nevertheless, in a season happily dominated by Auto-Union, Caracciola notched up two victories, in the Monaco and the Tunis Grands Prix.

Out of the disaster of 1936 came the great success of 1937. For that year, and with a new Grand Prix formula in prospect, Daimler-Benz developed a completely new chassis and suspensions, incorporating an oval tube chassis frame, different and altogether longer-travel coil-spring front suspension, a longer wheelbase, and dramatically improved road "manners." The motor-racing authorities, however, made a thorough botch of their decision-making process, and having announced the new 1937 formula in February 1936, rescinded it in September, and extended the original formula for another season. Undaunted, Daimler-Benz fitted an enlarged and physically longer eight-cylinder engine, this time with a displacement of 345.37cu in (5.66 liters) and, for the first time, fitted with a supercharger which sucked fuel-air mixture from an "upstream" carburetor rather than blowing out air into a "down-stream" unit. This was significantly more efficient, and the race engines could always be relied upon to produce about 600bhp—which makes them the most powerful Grand Prix engines ever to have appeared in a race, before or since. Thus the W125, the most "classic" of all Daimler-Benz racing cars, and one which was destined to be used for only one year, came into existence.

The car itself was matched by a peerless team of drivers: Caracciola, von Brauchitsch, Hermann Lang, Christian Kautz and Dick Seaman. Between them and helped by good roadholding and a top speed which could certainly exceed 210mph (338km/h) if the gearing was right, they won seven out of the 13 events actually entered, and were always competitive and right up with the leaders in every event where they were beaten. The cars were thunderous, awe-inspiring, yet remarkably tractable monsters, and used that very special brand of alcohol-based fuel which gave rise to a completely unique and distinctive exhaust aroma, a smell of which could make grown men go weak at the knees, and a whiff of which, years later, would bring back all the memories of that remarkable 1937 season.

In 1938 and 1939, however, Daimler-Benz had a different Formula to deal

Left: The famous W125 Mercedes-Benz Grand Prix car of 1937.

Far left below: In spite of its powerful 345.37cu in (5.66-liter) eight-cylinder engine, the W125 Grand Prix car was a compact design which handled surprisingly well.

Below left: The front suspension of the 1937 W125 car was independent and the brake drums filled the big wire wheels.

1937 Type W125 Grand Prix Car

Engine: Eight cylinders, in line, in nine-bearing steel cylinder block with integral heads, and light-alloy crankcase. Bore and stroke, capacity: 3.70×4.01in, 345.4cu in (94×102mm, 5660cc). Nondetachable steel cylinder head in unit with block. Four overhead valves per cylinder, opposed at 60 degrees, operated by twin overhead camshafts with interposed finger rockers. Dry sump lubrication. One triple-choke Mercedes-Benz carburetor, and one Roots supercharger with front-mounted engine. Open propeller providing 12psi boost. Maximum power: (best engine) 646bhp at 5800rpm; average engines gave about 600bhp.

Transmission: Single-dry-plate clutch in unit shaft to four-speed all-indirect manual gearbox without synchromesh, in unit with chassis-mounted spiral-bevel final drive. Remote-control right-hand gear change. Exposed universally jointed drive shafts to rear wheels.

Chassis: Separate tubular steel chassis frame with oval tube side-members and tubular cross-bracings. Light-alloy single-seater body shell with exposed wheels. Independent front suspension by coil springs and wishbones. De Dion rear suspension by torsion bars with radius arms, and with sliding block of De Dion tube. Lever-arm hydraulic dampers. Steering wheel removable for access. Worm-and-nut steering. Four-wheel hydraulically operated drum brakes, all outboard. Center-lock 17in wire wheels. Front tires: 5.25×17in, rear tires: 7×19in, 7×22in or 7×24in depending on gearing required.

Dimensions: Wheelbase: 9ft 2in (2.79m). Front track: 4ft 10in (1.47m), rear track: 4ft 7in (1.40m). Overall length: (approx) 13ft 6in (4.11m). Unladen weight: 1837lb (833kg).

with. Although the company might well have retired after 1937, if it had only had its own fortunes to consider, it was now a matter of national (Nazi-inspired) pride that German cars should continue to be dominant in international motorsport. Both Daimler-Benz and Auto-Union, therefore, designed new cars with which to fight each other, for the opposition from Italy and France had now fallen away.

Auto-Union's 1938/1939 car was still mid-engined but had a supercharged V12 cylinder engine and, more important, it had much improved roadholding. Furthermore, from mid-1938 it also had the undoubtedly remarkable services of Tazio Nuvolari as a driver. To match this car and to meet the requirements of a complex formula which allowed engines of up to 274.6cu in (4.5 liters) (unsupercharged) or 183.1cu in (3.0 liters) (supercharged), with a minimum (not maximum) weight of 1873lb (850kg), Max Sailer's Daimler-Benz designers decided to evolve a new supercharged engine and related transmission, which was to be fitted to the W125-type chassis and suspensions. The result was the W154.

Even while the 1653lb (750kg) Formula had been in progress, large V12 and V16 engines had been designed at Stuttgart-Unterturkheim (the V16s never appeared though the V12s were used in record cars, described later in this chapter). For the 1938 formula, Daimler-Benz designers actually asked Dr Porsche's design bureau to design a 274.6cu in (4.5-liter) engine for them — when Porsche returned, it was to propose a V24 cylinder layout! — but eventually they settled for a V12 layout of their own. This was fitted with a slightly angled transmission line, so that the driving seat could be placed alongside rather than above the line of the propeller shaft.

Except that it was a V12 instead of a straight-eight engine, the 2.6 × 2.8in (67 × 70mm), 180.7cu in (2962cc) M154 unit was typically Daimler-Benz in every way. In original 1938 form it produced more than 468bhp at the very high speed of 7800rpm; by the end of 1939 when improved, refined and fitted with two-stage supercharging, this figure had been raised to more than 480bhp at a slightly lower engine speed. Because the W154/M163 (there never was, officially, a W163 *car* as such) had such good roadholding, it was almost as fast on some circuits as the more powerful W125 had been.

In this formula the greatly improved V12 Auto-Unions were more competitive than before, but Mercedes-Benz results were still outstanding. Although Tazio Nuvolari's Auto-Union car won in Italy and in Britain, there were six major W154 victories to celebrate, in which all the team drivers, Lang, von Brauchitsch, Seaman and Caracciola shared the spoils. In 1939 the W154/M163 team, quite literally, were the best by a considerable margin, and Hermann Lang was the most successful driver. Team cars won five major events including Pau, Eifel, Belgium, Germany and Switzerland, all but one of them going to Lang. It was, however, a tragic year also, for Dick Seaman crashed badly in the Belgian Grand Prix at Spa, was severely burned in the fire which followed, and never recovered; it was the first team fatality for some years, and cast a gloom over the whole proceedings. Even as the Second World War was breaking out, Daimler-Benz was winning a round-the-houses race in Belgrade, but after that all forms of motorsport had to be called off.

In the meantime, however, Daimler-Benz had pulled off one quite remarkable *coup*. The organizers of that most glamorous of 1930s races, the Grand Prix of Tripoli, who had strong and obvious Italian sympathies, became so furious at the continued domination of their event by German teams that they decided to run the 1939 event with 91.5cu in (1.5-liter) cars, where Italian designers were very strong. In September 1938 (when they judged that it would be far too late for the Germans to do anything about it), they and other Italian

organizers announced that their 1939 event would be limited to 91.5cu in (1.5-liter) cars only. The Tripoli race would be held in May, less than eight months after the announcement.

The organizers were only partly successful—Auto-Union decided not to build cars, but Daimler-Benz, who by now was becoming convinced of its own supremacy, thought it could; in less than eight months, two entirely new V8-engined 91.5cu in (1.5-liter) W165s were built, tested, and won the event! Sailer commanded that work should be started as soon as he heard about the change in rules, by February 1939 all the drawings had been finished, and in April the first car was tested at Hockenheim.

The rest of the story is history and Daimler-Benz legend. Two of the little "W154 look-alike" W165s, complete with very similar chassis engineering and with 265bhp 91.2cu in (1495cc) engines, were taken to Tripoli, where Hermann Lang finished first and Rudolph Caracciola finished second. The Italians were outclassed and humiliated, and the meticulous planning and pre-race testing by Daimler-Benz was amply justified. Three cars had been built, but none of them was ever used "in anger" again.

It was the end of an era, not only in sporting, but in political terms as well. Never again would the world of motor racing have the pleasure and the great excitement of seeing two dedicated and well-financed German Grand Prix teams battling it out on the race tracks of the world. One is almost tempted to call this a "Golden" Age of motor racing, except that in view of the color of the cars, it perhaps ought to be a "Silver" Age instead.

RECORD BREAKING

As an aside from motor racing around circuits or competition in speed hill climbs, Daimler-Benz also found time to build a series of cars for straight-line record attempts, and it would not be right to present a full history of the marque without mentioning these. Not since Héméry's Brooklands attempts before the First World War had the company or its ancestors been interested, but in the 1934–1939 period record runs became almost annual occurrences.

It started quietly enough in October 1934, when two W25s were taken to a new concrete road near Gyon, close to Budapest, and where one car with a single-seater "sedan" bubble top achieved a two-way 197.35mph (317.54km/h). In 1936, however, a much more ambitious project was mounted, in which a 616bhp Type DAB 341.7cu in (5.6-liter) V12 engine (originally conceived for the Grand Prix cars but found to be grossly overweight) was matched to a redundant W25 chassis, and an experimental full-width streamlined body style. On 26 October Rudi Caracciola set standing start records, and two-way speeds of up to 228mph (367km/h), on a new section of autobahn just south of Frankfurt alongside the site of what is now the international airport.

In May 1937, as a diversion, a team of cars was entered for the race on the very fast Avus road circuit—a circuit to which a dramatically steep and fast bank had been added at the north turn. Streamlined cars were built for von Brauchitsch (with a DAB V12), Hermann Lang (W25 with M125 engine) and Rudi Caracciola (W125), while Dick Seaman had a normal unstreamlined W125. No other car, not even the special Auto-Unions, could live with the team; Caracciola won the first seven-lap heat, and von Brauchitsch the second, while Hermann Lang cruised round to win the final after other cars struck

Top: On a very wet Spa circuit, Richard Seaman crashed his W154 183.1cu in (3.0-liter) Grand Prix car when leading the 1939 Belgian Grand Prix, and tragically lost his life in the fire which followed.

Bottom: Hermann Lang urges the "one race—one victory" W165 91.5cu in (1.5-liter) model towards the finish of the 1939 Tripoli Grand Prix.

trouble. His race average of 162.61mph (261.64km/h), was a world record for the next 20 years. During that weekend, however, both Caracciola and Lang discovered that their cars' aerodynamics were not perfect, as the noses were lifting, and stability was affected.

It was such lift which affected the performance of the Mercedes-Benz record cars at the official Record Week on the Frankfurt autobahn in October 1937. The problem was so serious at first that great dents appeared in the upper panel of the Mercedes-Benz's nose due to low air pressure at that point. Changes had to be made in a great hurry and lead weights added to the front of the car before Caracciola achieved 248mph (399km/h). However, by this time Rosemeyer's Auto-Union had clocked 252mph (405km/h). Honors at this point were even.

The W154 Mercedes-Benz Grand Prix car of 1938 and 1939 had a supercharged 183.1cu in (3.0-liter) V12 engine and in its final form developed more than 480hp.

On 28 January 1938 on the same stretch of road, Caracciola and Daimler-Benz avenged their defeat of three months earlier. A revised body style, which dispensed with air inlets to a radiator (cooling was ensured by a water/ice tank inside which the normal radiator sat) helped the car to achieve a splendid 268.7mph (432.3km/h) for the two-way kilometer, helped along by the fact that the DAB V12 now produced a staggering 736bhp at 5800rpm. Later that morning Auto-Union and Bernd Rosemeyer attempted to regain their title with appalling results. Hit by a sudden cross wind as the car rushed under an autobahn bridge, Rosemeyer lost control, the car flew off the road, and the brilliant little driver was killed instantly.

In one final appearance by a record car based on a Grand Prix car, Rudi Caracciola journeyed to the new autobahn between Dessau and Bitterfeld in north Germany to try out a car which was, in effect, a 1938 W154 chassis and engine with a specially streamlined body. Attempting class D [183.1cu in (3.0-liter) records] it achieved 248.3mph (399.5km/h), quite enough to smash existing records, and also set standing-kilometer records at 110.2mph (177.3km/h).

The most monstrous, and the most exciting, of all Daimler-Benz record cars

*Hermann Lang, a Daimler-Benz employee as
well as a racing driver, was the complete
master of the 183.1cu in (3.0-liter) W154 Grand
Prix cars in 1939.*

never appeared in public when it was newly built, and its existence only became
known in the course of the occupation of Germany by Allied troops in 1945.
This was the Type 80 model, built with only one object in mind—to take the
Land Speed Record from the British.

The project started in a discussion between Auto-Union "works" racing
driver Hans Stuck and Dr Porsche in 1936. Once Sir Malcolm Campbell had
left the record at 301mph (484km/h) in 1935, Stuck developed an obsession to
beat him. The fact that first George Eyston and then John Cobb progressively
raised the mark to 369mph (594km/h) did not deter him. By then Stuck and
Porsche knew that Daimler-Benz was developing the very modern and very
powerful inverted V12 Type DB600 series aero-engines, so they approached
the company for an engine.

At the end of 1936 Daimler-Benz management and engineers agreed to
supply an engine and to build the car to Professor Porsche's designs, but added
that they could not possibly finish the car before the end of 1937. However,
progress was slow, and even though Daimler-Benz agreed to supply a 2500bhp
2068.6cu in (33.9-liter) DB601 engine, intensive work on the 1938 Grand Prix
cars meant that the car was still not finished by the end of 1938. In the meantime Eyston and Cobb had been dueling away on the Utah Salt Flats with such
ferocity that the record had been raised to 357mph (574km/h), at which point
Dr Porsche realized that more power would be needed. He asked for, and got, a
2715.4cu in (44.5-liter) Type DB603V3, which might eventually produce
3000bhp, and one of these units was duly fitted to the Type 80 early in 1939.

It looked bizarre, but it also looked right. The vast aero-engine was mid-
mounted, as in the Auto-Union Grand Prix cars, and the massive chassis
supported two pairs of driven rear wheels. The strange but all-enveloping body
(which even has a few "family" resemblances to the sports-racing Porsches of
the 1960s, the author feels) housed its driver almost between the front wheels,
and at each side of the streamlined body there was a large fixed airfoil section,
set to give six degrees of negative incidence and a large and guaranteed
quantity of aerodynamic down force. Its total weight, with driver installed,
was about 6660lb (3021kg), and its projected maximum speed was to be more
than 600km/h (or more than 373mph).

Nothing, it seemed, was too much for this car, for the Nazi party even
arranged for the dual carriageway autobahn at Dessau to be converted into a
wide concrete single carriageway track for the Type 80's use. (It was not
thought advisable to take the Type 80 to the Utah Salt Flats in view of the
international situation.)

Although the chassis ran on a dynamometer for the first time in October
1939, the car never ventured out on to the road, and never made its attempt on
the Land Speed Record. Even though it miraculously escaped destruction
from Allied bombing during the Second World War, any value it might have
had was lost in the postwar confusion at Daimler-Benz, and by the fact that
John Cobb raised the record to 394mph (634km/h) in 1947. Even when the
project was new, and when Stuck's enthusiasm was boundless, there was
always a niggling doubt that the power available might not have been enough.
Now, we shall never know.

In any case, by the time the existence of the Type 80 record car became
known, Daimler-Benz was fighting for its very survival, after a war which had
been catastrophic for both Germany and itself.

6. REVIVAL AND EXPANSION

The war which engulfed Europe from 1939 to 1945 brought terrible destruction to almost every company and every industry on the continent. In Germany Daimler-Benz was always a prime target for bombing as it was one of the leading industrial complexes in the nation and was particularly noted for the building of a fine series of aero-engines. Two weeks of bombing in the fall of 1944 left much of the business in ruins, and in the process Daimler-Benz's famous motoring heritage was effectively wiped out.

Things were so bad and the destruction so complete that Daimler-Benz directors were obliged to issue a terse statement to the effect that: ". . . for all practical purposes Daimler-Benz has ceased to exist. . . ."—and they were not exaggerating. At least 70 percent of the old Stuttgart-Unterturkheim factory had been destroyed along with 80 percent of the truck works at Gaggenau and no less than 85 percent of the vast Sindelfingen factory just outside the city.

In one respect, however, Daimler-Benz was somewhat fortunate: when the fighting at last came to an end and when the great armies stopped sweeping across the land, most of the factories and the business found themselves in West Germany and part of what promised to be a free world. The Marienfelde factory in Berlin had been bombed out, but what remained of it was dismantled and shipped off to Russia. BMW, by comparison, suffered very badly because its principal assembly plant at Eisenach found itself hidden away behind Russian lines, and would never be returned to its rightful owners.

It was quite impossible, however, for Daimler-Benz to begin building private cars again in 1945, even if authorization had been given. For month after weary month, therefore, as the employees of Daimler-Benz gradually returned to their old jobs, their immediate task was simply to clear up the mess. Managers worked alongside assembly staff, and technicians worked alongside maintenance specialists, all concentrating on preparing the ground for what they all sensed as the rebirth of a world-famous concern.

Clearly, at this stage, there was no possibility of designing, tooling up, and manufacturing a series of new models—nor even one new model. Even in North America, which had been physically untouched by the fighting, there were few postwar models before 1948; in Germany there was not only great destruction to be swept aside, but there was financial chaos. Thus it was out of the question.

At first, therefore, all activities concentrated on the repair and maintenance of existing cars and commercial vehicles. By the time that enough space had been made available for limited production of cars to recommence, the directors had taken the decision to concentrate on only one model—the prewar Type 170V. Even if the tooling had not been destroyed, the financial and social climate ruled out any possibility of building the fast and massive 540K tourers and coupes, or of making even a few of the prestigious and elephantine 770 Grosser models.

Somehow, in the face of incredible difficulties, the first of the 170V engines, a 103.7cu in (1.7-liter) four-cylinder unit, was finished in February 1946, and the first complete car was built in June. It was an uphill struggle, for even though early production concentrated on making cars for the police, for ambulance use, and even for lightweight delivery work, only 214 cars were built before the end of 1946, and just over a thousand were assembled in 1947. The currency reforms of 1948, stabilization of government, and the establishment of a rehabilitation policy helped bring about a transformation in national outlook. Supplies became more easily available, more people could afford to buy cars, and this, together with the continued rebuilding of the factories, meant that more than 5000 cars were sold in 1948, and that a total of 17,417 followed in 1949. By that

Previous page: One symbol of postwar rebirth, was this 300 Cabriolet of the early 1950s, with end-to-end engineering innovation. This car was always known as Fritz Nallinger's personal project.

Right: By the mid-1960s Daimler-Benz had a wide and extremely prestigious range of cars, and had introduced two different overhead-camshaft V8 engine designs. In the foreground is a 280SE 3.5 and by the door of the mansion is the (comparatively) "short" Mercedes-Benz 600 limousine.

time the first of the postwar cars was ready for production, and a real explosion of sales got under way.

There has been much talk for many years and in many walks of life, about the "Economic Miracle" achieved by West Germany in the 1950s and 1960s, and this was nowhere more apparent than in the fortunes of Daimler-Benz. Working with great energy, and with single-minded application, the company not only managed to repair and rebuild its factories, but to expand them mightily. Starting from scratch in 1945, they pushed up their production of passenger cars to more than 40,000 in 1951, to nearly 100,000 in 1958, and to 200,000 in 1967. In the same period they re-entered every market sector already familiar to them, covering everything from the diesel-engined taxi market to the exclusive and very restricted prestige car market, from 103.7cu in (1.7-liter) four-cylinder diesel engines to 384.4cu in (6.3-liter) fuel-injected V8 overhead camshaft engines, from 38bhp to 250bhp, and from cars weighing 2500lb (1134kg) to vast limousines weighing nearly 6000lb (2722kg). Maximum speeds swept up from the modest 67mph (108km/h) of the 1946 models to the 165mph (265km/h) claimed for the first of the 300SL coupes. At the same time, Daimler-Benz redeveloped and intensified its production and sales of commercial vehicles and other non-passenger car products, and, for several years in the 1950s, returned to motor racing with almost complete, and overwhelming success.

The many and varied phases in the evolution of the postwar cars, effectively culminated in the mid-1960s when the engineers and directors paused briefly, took a deep corporate breath, and began to plan their technical assault on the

Left: One of the myriad "S" class cars built at the end of the 1960s and the beginning of the 1970s was the 300SEL 4.5, which indicates that it had a 4.5-liter (274.6cu in) V8 engine, and was a long-wheelbased version of the basic design.

Left below: When the smaller of the two new V8 engines of the 1960s was squeezed into an engine bay for which it was not originally designed, there was little space to spare.

Below: Neat and up-to-the minute styling touches, in detail, of the 300SEL 4.5 shows the paired headlights which allowed the car to be imported into North America without modification.

1970s. It is the author's opinion that the "New Generation" models revealed in 1968 were the first of the modern wave, and it is with those cars that he opens Chapter 8 on the "Modern Times" of Daimler-Benz.

Postwar rebirth, recovery and consolidation, therefore, covers about 20 years. It begins with the building up, mainly by hand, of the prewar type 170V models in 1946, and ends in the late 1960s after the successful launch of the Type W108/W109 "S" class cars and at the maturity of the 230SL sporting models. In that time, although most of the production and a great deal of the profit came from building high-quality four-door sedan cars for the conservative and fast-growing middle-class and executive market, a lot of the glamor came from the building, in more limited numbers, of cars as exotic as the gull-wing 300SL coupes, as self-indulgent as the 220SE and 300SE convertibles, or as splendid and self-important as the huge 600 Limousines and Pullmans which graced the range in the 1960s and 1970s.

To browse through a completely cataloged list of Mercedes-Benz models built in this period is to risk becoming thoroughly confused, and to wonder whether any type of logic actually existed at Stuttgart in this period. The first state would be understandable, but the second judgment would be quite unjustified. Perhaps more than any other European car manufacturer of the period, Daimler-Benz knew exactly how it could generate the maximum customer interest, and the most sales, by the skillful combination of basic body shells, coachbuilt derivatives of them, and the ever-widening range of engines which they were building. Perhaps the most extreme example of this came as late as 1968, when the 300SEL 6.3 came along, in which the bulky V8 engine

from the 600 Limousine had somehow been squeezed into the 300SEL's body shell. It was, at the time, the ultimate in "Q-cars" and led to one German magazine publishing a cartoon of a Daimler-Benz engineer vainly trying to thrust a aero-engine into the engine bay of a 300SEL, while saying between gritted teeth: "It's just *got* to go in. . . ."

Postwar production started on the basis of building cars with separate tubular chassis frames and separate steel bodies, and even the first completely new postwar model, the fast and luxurious Type 300 of 1951, remained true to this type of construction. The first-ever Mercedes-Benz model with a unit-construction pressed-steel body shell was the Type 180 of 1953, the first of a wide range of models built until 1965, which included several different engines, and which also gave rise to the 190SL sports tourer. In the meantime, too, the esoteric and very special 300SL had been revealed, but it had little commercial significance.

By the end of the 1950s Daimler-Benz was not only ready to offer a new unit-construction body as the basis of yet more complex model subdivisions (destined to replace not only the 1954 vintage shell but to take over from the 300s which were the last to retain the large-tube frames), but the company had also perfected the use of gasoline injection. The be-finned range of 1959–1968, always known within the factory as the Type W111/W112 cars, was a really versatile advance.

In the early 1960s the Type 600, like the 300SL of the 1950s, was good for company morale, great for publicity, and ideal for a particular and rather

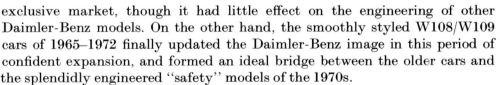

Left: The Mercedes 300 of the early 1950s, designed after the reconstruction of Daimler-Benz had been tackled, was the company's flagship for some years.

Below: Although the styling of the early-1950s Type 300 was completely new, there were obvious similarities to the last Mercedes-Benz models of the late 1930s.

exclusive market, though it had little effect on the engineering of other Daimler-Benz models. On the other hand, the smoothly styled W108/W109 cars of 1965–1972 finally updated the Daimler-Benz image in this period of confident expansion, and formed an ideal bridge between the older cars and the splendidly engineered "safety" models of the 1970s.

I am convinced that in a book of this nature it is not at all appropriate to plow carefully and unerringly through every type, category and subdivision of the quantity-production sedan cars, but I am also sure that their most important new features must be noted. This, therefore, is not the place to show why a 220a is very different from a 220, why a 219 of 1956 is by no means the same type of car as a 220S of 1959, or why a 300SEL of 1967 should have an oversquare engine of 170.9cu in (2.8-liters) while the 300SE of 1961 which it replaced should have an undersquare 183.1cu in (3.0-liter) unit. There are dictionaries and definitions of this type which prove just how complex a piece of analysis this would be.

In one way, at least, the wholesale destruction of war was a great spur to Daimler-Benz to rebuild its entire image, and its supply of power units in particular. Starting from the humble little 103.5cu in (1697cc) gasoline and diesel engines of 1946, the company progressively developed new four-cylinder gasoline and diesel engines spanning the 115.9 to 140.3cu in (1.9 to 2.3 liter) ranges, a complex 183.1cu in (3.0-liter) "six" which found especial fame in the 300SL, and another "six" which began its life in 1951 and was still very effective in the 1970s. In 20 years the firm produced so many subdivisions of

Left: The 300 Cabriolet of the early 1950s with – unusually – a four-door style. The chassis was of an all-independent oval-tube design.

Left below: The 300 Cabriolet of the 1950s exemplified everything about Daimler-Benz which was connected with careful detailed styling, massive construction, and great attention to a high quality finish.

This 300 of the early 1950s looks new – which is remarkable as the shot was taken in 1980

these three ranges, some with different cylinder bores, some with different strokes, and all with single overhead camshaft valve gear, that there was no corner of its ambition which could not adequately be covered. Although twin-cam engines and a new generation of V8 engines made all the news in the early 1970s, and even though new four-cylinder units have been revealed for the 1980s, some Daimler-Benz models still use the descendants of this far-sighted enterprise of the 1950s.

The first few postwar years were dominated by the building of 170V/170S/170D models, which were all prewar in spirit if not in construction. Daimler-Benz, in the meantime, was working away on a new car which might recapture the great days of the 1930s, and when it appeared in 1951 it was seen to be a fine and fast 183.1cu in (3.0-liter) machine. The 300 model, and especially its very impressive convertible derivative, the 300S, was exactly the type of car which a company fighting to regain respectability needed. Although it retained a tubular chassis frame with oval-section tubes, and had styling which was only half way between the prewar shape of the 170s and the squared-up style of the 220as which would soon follow, many mechanical features were dazzlingly modern. Not only did the new Type 300 have an all-new six-cylinder engine, gearbox and hypoid bevel final drive, but it also had driver-operated electrical control over auxiliary torsion bars at the rear suspension, designed to stiffen it up under load. What transpired was that this had been Fritz Nallinger's pet project for some time (almost to the extent that he delegated all responsibility for other designs to his subordinates for a time), and that he was determined to demonstrate that Daimler-Benz was still capable of designing and building technically sophisticated and successful cars.

And so it was. The 300, even though it was not a particularly modern style when first seen in 1951, and certainly outdated by the time it was dropped in 1962, sold to the tune of 11,430 examples, even though it was much the most

Above: The 300S two-door Roadster, a prestige car which handled and performed better than any previous Mercedes-Benz model.

Above right: The 300S Roadster was an indulgence for any owner, for its seating capacity had been sacrificed to good looks and a cavernous luggage compartment.

Below right: The 300S Roadster was effectively a modern interpretation of the type of cars for which Daimler-Benz were noted in the 1930s, such as the 540K models. In this instance, however, no supercharger was needed.

Right: Room for a mountain of expensive luggage for wealthy owners of the 1950s' 300S Roadster.

Right: The 300S Coupe was like the Roadster, but had a stylish fixed roof.

Right below: The 300S Coupe was one of the most desirable Daimler-Benz products of the early 1950s.

Below: Clearly the 300S Coupe shares most of its coachbuilt body shell with that of the Roadster.

Far left: The 300SL road car was a direct development of the racing prototypes used so successfully by Daimler-Benz in 1952. The grille behind the front wheels was for engine-bay cooling.

Below left: The classic "gull-wing" 300SL model. Access to the seats was never easy, but as the performance was quite outstanding, few people complained!

Left: Inside the cockpit of the 300SL, the steering wheel folded down to provide easier entry and exit for the driver.

expensive car in West Germany, and in the Daimler-Benz range, throughout that time.

The most outstanding feature, and one which was to have important sporting and even racing connotations, was the engine itself. Apart from the accumulated experience of many engineers, there was no historical link between this engine and any of the great power units of the 1930s. In general layout, with a cast-iron block and a light-alloy head, it was conventional enough, and even the chain-driven overhead camshaft layout had been seen before, but it was the detail of the unit which was so enthralling. The cylinder head had a completely flat face at the cylinder-head joint, and all the combustion chamber was formed in the top of the pistons by an angled block/face joint. There were two lines of valves, operated through fingers under the camshaft, and the spark plugs were inserted through the side of the cylinder block into the preformed combustion chamber. Even in original form, it produced 115bhp with the aid of twin dual choke Solex carburetors, but by the time the 300SL had been blooded, and the fuel injection systems had been proven, the 300D's power output was up to 160bhp (DIN) at 5300rpm, while retaining the original 182.8cu in (2996cc) engine size.

Even though it was a fine car, therefore, the Type 300 was more important for the car it spawned—the 300SL—than for its own record. The original conception of the 300SL two-seater sports coupe is described in more detail in the next chapter, and at this point it is merely necessary to show that it used many Type 300 components—engine, transmission, rear axle and even suspension components—in rather modified form, all housed in a sensationally modern multi-tube space-frame type of chassis, topped off by a sleek and futuristic coupe body style which incorporated lift-up "gull-wing" doors, which had virtually been forced on the engineers by the restrictions and the great depth of the multi-tube frame.

The original racing 300SLs used a much-modified Type 300 engine, laid well over onto its side and still retaining carburetors for the supply of fuel/air mixture. For the production car, however, which made its public bow in the spring of 1954 but did not truly get into quantity production until 1955, a fuel-injected derivative was developed. This was done by designing new cylinder heads incorporating spark-plug access, and by using the original spark-plug apertures in the cylinder wall to house the injector nozzles. Daimler-Benz's great experience in developing fuel-injected derivatives of their aero-engines helped a lot, and the 300SL became the first-ever production car to be put on sale with fuel-injection as standard equipment.

It is only fair to posterity to admit that the handling of the 300SL could be downright disconcerting in certain conditions—the combination of high

Left: The beautiful lines and features of the 300SL "gull-wing," which was produced between 1954 and 1957. Maximum speeds of up to 165mph (264km/h) were claimed, depending on the gearing chosen.

1954 Type 300SL "Gull-wing" Coupe

Engine: Six cylinders, in line, in seven-bearing cast-iron block, installed in car at an angle of 50 degrees. Bore and stroke, capacity: 3.35×3.46in, 182.8cu in (85×88mm, 2996cc). Detachable light-alloy cylinder head with angled joint face between head and cylinder block. Combustion chamber formed in top of piston and corner of cylinder block. Two overhead valves per cylinder, staggered (one line of inlets, one line of exhausts), and operated by rockers from a single overhead camshaft. Dry-sump lubrication. Bosch direct fuel injection. Maximum power: 215bhp (net) at 5800rpm.

Transmission: Single-dry-plate clutch and four-speed all-synchromesh manual gearbox, both in unit with front-mounted engine. Remote control, central gearchange. Open propeller shaft to chassis-mounted hypoid-bevel final drive. Exposed, universally jointed drive shafts to rear wheels.

Chassis: Separate multi-tubular space frame, with many small-diameter steel tubes linking points of stress. Lightweight steel (some cars in light-alloy) two-seater body shell, with closed coupe style, and lift-up "gull-wing" doors. Independent front suspension by coil springs and wishbones. Independent rear suspension by coil springs, swing axles and radius arms. Telescopic dampers. Steering wheel hinged for access to driving seat, and steering by recirculating ball. Four-wheel hydraulically operated drum brakes, with vacuum-servo assistance. Pressed-steel 15in road wheels. Tires 6.70×15in.

Dimensions: Wheelbase: 7ft 10.5in. Front track: 4ft 7in (1.40m), rear track: 4ft 9in (1.45m). Overall length: 15ft 0in (4.57m). Unladen weight: 3000lb (1364kg).

speeds, high-pivot-type swing-axle rear suspension, and the cross-ply tires of the day all contributed to the over-steering problem — but if the right technique was applied (and very skilled drivers soon acquired it) it could be a truly fast car and a winner in races and rallies. Its designation of 300SL, where the "SL" effectively meant "Sports Lightweight" certainly applied to its bulk — a 300SL "gull-wing" weighed about 2850lb (1293kg) — but it did not mean that it was a fragile machine. It might have looked fragile to those not completely familiar with the engineering, but it must be stressed that any car which can win at Le Mans, over a 24-hour race, and in the roughest of rallies like Liège–Rome–Liège, must be a remarkably rugged machine.

Even in standard production form, and with the original 215bhp (DIN) engine, the "gull-wing" 300SL could be a fearsomely rapid machine. A variety of axle ratios were available, and in one condition the factory claimed a maximum speed approaching 165mph (265km/h). Nothing remotely approaching this speed was available on any other road car than the occasional (and very hand-built) Ferrari, and no other fast car of even similar performance was backed by any sort of service network which approached that of Daimler-Benz.

In 1955, 867 300SL "gull-wings" were built, but it was already clear to management that there were difficulties in selling a car which was rather difficult to get into and out of, almost impossible to park close to a wall

In "gull-wing" or Roadster form, there was no mistaking the sleek and exclusive lines of the 300SL two-seater sports car. It was one of the very fastest road cars in production during the 1950s.

because of the space required to swing up the doors, and one which rapidly let in the rain if the door was kept open in inclement weather for any length of time. The question of immodest entry or exit for ladies was never mentioned, though it was assuredly noted. For 1957, therefore, the controversial "gull-wing" layout was abandoned, and the 300SL Roadster style was brought into production in its place. Changes were made to the multi-tube frame, the height of the door sills was reduced, and conventional doors, front-hinged, were included in a conventional open two-seater roadster style, for which an optional, detachable, hardtop was available. The aerodynamics of the new car were not as favorable as the "gull-wing" style, but the Roadster could still nudge 155mph (249km/h) with the right gearing, and it was still one of the very fastest road cars in the world. The Roadster's engine had perhaps ten extra horsepower to its credit, but a much more significant improvement was that new low-pivot swing axle rear suspension was adopted, along with a compensator coil spring above the differential linking the two casings; this allowed the rear suspension to be softer in roll than in bump, which is always desirable, and it helped tame the original 300SL's rather unruly cornering habits. Low-pivot swing axles had been fitted to the unit-construction 220s from 1954, but this was the first-ever Daimler-Benz application of the compensating spring principle.

Unhappily for the romantics, the rather less dramatically styled 300SL Roadster was commercially more successful. The "gull-wing" had been in production for only three years, and 1400 units had been sold—the Roadster stayed in production for six years, and sold to the tune of 1858 cars.

While all this excitement was going on, and while Daimler-Benz was initiating a very successful Grand Prix racing program, the 190SL Roadster was introduced. It was something of a paradox. Although it was never a very specially engineered car (it was, after all, built up on the floor pan and mechanical components of the Type 180 sedan) it was in production from 1955 to 1963, could be guaranteed to exceed 100mph (160km/h) in most conditions, and sold nearly 26,000 examples. It never attracted the attention of the 300SL, with which it was always concurrent, and was never intended to be a competition car, but was an obvious and lasting success.

It was these exciting cars and the introduction of features like Bosch fuel injection on the middle-class 220SE (with the well-established 180-type of body shell) which helped bring the reputation of Daimler-Benz to a new peak in the 1950s, but the withdrawal from motor racing at the end of 1955 meant that the company could devote even more attention to the development of new touring cars for the 1960s. This led, in 1959, to the announcement of the first of the W111/W112 cars, now recognized by all Mercedes-Benz enthusiasts by the sharp but small tail fins, and by the vertical styling of the headlight/indicator clusters. The range not only embraced all the low-powered diesel-engined cars which meant so much to the expansion of Mercedes-Benz sales, but eventually stretched up to the original lengthened-wheelbase 300SEL of 1963–1967. Not only was the camber-compensating rear suspension adopted, but on the 300SE and 300SEL models there was self-leveling high-pressure air suspension in place of conventional coil springs.

The two cars which caught the public's attention, however—and both were revealed in 1963—were the sleek and individually styled 230SL sports car, and the vast but highly effective Type 600 limousine. Both, in their individual ways, emphasized that the rebuilding of Daimler-Benz was now complete and that the German firm was once again ready and able to build some of the best-engineered cars in the world. However, although the 230SL was the sort of car which observers might have been led to expect if they had only thought about it, the magnificent Type 600 was a real surprise. In those days there was not the amount of pre-release ferreting round for "scoop" information that there is today, and so the Type 600, when first seen at the 1963 Frankfurt Motor Show, caused a real sensation.

It was, in every way, a worthy successor to the Grosser Mercedes models of the 1930s, and was considerably more complex than any previous Daimler-Benz product. Except for the fact that even the "short" (ie, the four-door six-window version) limousine was 18ft 2in (5.54m) long, while the longer eight-window Pullman was 20ft 6in (6.25m) long, the Type 600 had a conventional unit-construction pressed-steel body/chassis unit. Its style was conventional by Daimler-Benz standards, though rather more squared up than one might have expected, and it was all suspended by wishbone independent front suspension and low-pivot swing-axle rear suspension. Like the 300SEL, however, it featured high-pressure air suspension with self-leveling controls, and naturally it was only to be supplied with Daimler-Benz's own brand of automatic transmission. The two really remarkable features of its design were the completely new and very carefully engineered 386.3cu in (6.3-liter) overhead camshaft V8 engine, which was rated at a very solid and understressed 250bhp, and the fact that so many controls were either power-assisted or were completely operated by hydraulic or electrical means. There was power-assisted steering, which was

Right: Mercedes-Benz 600 models were rare; long-wheelbase models were even rarer; and those with Landaulette styles were the most exclusive of all. This car had a mere four doors, but a six-door version was also available if one insisted.
(Coys of Kensington Collection)

Center: The huge and impressive lines of the three-ton 600 Landaulette, built in 1975 as a "Head of State" model.
(Coys of Kensington Collection)

Below: When launched in 1963, the 386.3cu in (6.3-liter) V8 engined Mercedes-Benz 600 limousine was the most complex car yet put on sale in Europe, and possibly in the world. Almost everything was either fully automatic or had power assistance.

Below right: Among the details standardized in the 600 model were hydraulically operated windows.

Above: This long-wheelbase 600 Pullman with a Landaulette body style was prepared for use by Pope Paul VI.

Top left: The special 600 Landaulette built for the use of Pope Paul VI in the 1960s had a single central rear seat, not unlike a throne.

Top right: The 600 was very large and very luxuriously equipped. Although it was surprisingly fast, it could also be driven impressively slowly for ceremonial occasions.

This is one of the "ultimate" 600 Pullmans, complete with six-door coachwork and almost every conceivable fitting, including television for the rear-seat passengers. The 386.3cu in (6.3-liter) engine almost filled the spacious under-hood space.

1963 Type 600 Limousine

Engine: Eight cylinders, in 90 degree "V" formation, in five-bearing cast-iron combined block/crankcase. Bore and stroke, capacity: 4.06×3.74in, 386.3cu in (103×95mm, 6332cc). Detachable light-alloy cylinder heads. Two overhead valves per cylinder, in line along each bank of cylinders, operated by single overhead camshaft per bank, with interposed finger-type rockers. Bosch indirect fuel injection into inlet ports. Maximum power: 250bhp (DIN) at 4000rpm.

Transmission: Daimler-Benz four-speed automatic transmission, incorporating fluid coupling, in unit with front-mounted engine. Remote, steering-column mounted, gear change. Open propeller shaft to chassis-mounted hypoid-bevel final drive, incorporating limited-slip device. Exposed, universally jointed drive shafts to rear wheels.

Chassis: Unit-construction pressed-steel body/chassis unit, in choice of wheelbases. Independent front suspension by high-pressure air suspension units and wishbones. Independent rear suspension by low-pivot swing axles, high-pressure air suspension units, radius arms, and self-leveling control. Telescopic dampers. Worm-and-nut steering with power assistance. Four-wheel hydraulically operated disk brakes, front and rear, with high-pressure power assistance. Bolt-on 15in pressed steel disk wheels. Tires: 9.00×15in.

Choice of four-door six-window, four-door eight-window, or six-door eight-window limousine/Pullman bodywork.

Dimensions: Wheelbase: 10ft 6in or 12ft 9.5in (3.20m or 3.90m). Front track: 5ft 2.5in (1.59m), rear track: 5ft 2.0in (1.57m). Overall length: 18ft 2in or 20ft 6in (5.54m or 6.25m).

Left: The last of the famous "pagoda roof" coupes built between 1963 and 1971 was the 280SL model.

Right: In the early and mid-1960s, tens of thousands of these 190D sedans, complete with four-cylinder diesel engines, were provided for use as taxis or rental cars.

Below left: The 230SL sports car replaced both the 190SL and 300SL models in 1963.

1963 Type 230SL Sports-Tourer

Engine: Six cylinders, in line, in seven-bearing cast-iron cylinder block. Bore and stroke, capacity: 3.23 × 2.87in, 140.7cu in (82 × 72.8mm, 2306cc). Light-alloy cylinder head. Two overhead valves per cylinder operated by finger-type rockers from single overhead camshaft. Indirect Bosch fuel injection into inlet ports. Maximum power: 170bhp (gross) at 5600rpm.

Transmission: Single-dry-plate clutch, and four-speed all-synchromesh manual gearbox, both in unit with front-mounted engine. Remote-control central change. Open propeller shaft to chassis-mounted hypoid-bevel final drive. Optional four-speed Daimler-Benz automatic transmission with fluid coupling. Exposed, universally jointed drive shafts to rear wheels.

Chassis: Unit-construction pressed-steel body/chassis unit, in two plus two open, convertible, or detachable fixed-head coupe styles. Independent front suspension by coil springs and wishbones. Independent rear suspension by low-pivot swing axles, coil springs, radius arms, and central compensating spring. Telescopic dampers. Recirculating ball steering, with optional power assistance. Four-wheel hydraulically operated brakes, front disks and rear drums, vacuum servo assisted. Steel 14in disk wheels. Tires: 185 × 14in.

Dimensions: Wheelbase: 7ft 10in (2.49m). Front track: 4ft 10.5in (1.51m), rear track: 4ft 10.5in (1.51m). Overall length: 14ft 1.5in (4.30m). Unladen weight: 2700lb (1224kg).

quite essential when the weight of the machine was considered, and there was also the hydraulic operation of seats, window lifts, door locks and the luggage compartment lid. There was high-pressure power braking for the four-wheel disk-brake installation; there was not one, but two, engine-driven alternators; and there was the option of full air-conditioning. It was widely suggested by the motoring press that this new car would deal a severe blow to Rolls-Royce (which proved to be quite untrue, especially as the British concern was preparing its own very advanced Silver Shadow for launch in 1965), and that it would almost become an essential "buy" for any self-respecting Middle East potentate, or for any true business tycoon.

When launching the big car, Daimler-Benz made it quite clear that it had engineered the Type 600 without much attention to costs, and that even the very high price of 56,500 DM (or 63,500 DM for the Pullman) — $19,500 and $24,000 respectively in the United States — was not enough to make it truly profitable to manufacture. They agreed that it was a car necessarily built with the prestige of the company and its customers, and the corporate image of the company in mind. It was not to be subjected to regular and unnecessary attacks of restyling, and it would always be a distinctly "quality-first" product.

Very few of the world's car makers could have got away with such an indulgence (and, in many cases, the stockholder would have been most unhappy at the prospect) but Daimler-Benz never seemed to be in any difficulty. First deliveries were made in 1964 and carried on at a steady rate until 1972, at which point the 600s became available only "to special order." Although sales at the rate achieved by Rolls-Royce in the 1960s were never achieved (a total of 345 Type 600s and 63 Pullmans were produced in 1965, the best year), more than 2000 600s and more than 400 Pullmans had been built and sold by the mid-1970s, by which time production was down to no more than 40 or 50 cars a year.

It might be said of splendid and wonderfully complex cars like the Type 600 Mercedes-Benz that, if they did not exist, then someone would have had to invent them, for there is always a small but discerning clientele who demand, and usually get, the best of everything. As to the car itself, it was almost as if Rudolf Uhlenhaut's engineers had been allowed to express their personality and expertise at a level otherwise not open to them. Another author has suggested that a Type 600 had a passenger compartment which was "an oasis of opulence, rampant with rolled and pleated leather . . . and a virtual forest of glistening burled walnut wainscotting and cabinetry." For a time, it was also the best-engineered car in the world, and there were many who thought that the Rolls-Royce Silver Shadow of 1965 merely came close to it.

Safety requirements of the 1970s could not spoil the rakish but typically Daimler-Benz lines of the 350SL which, in 1971, replaced the long-running 230/250/280SL range.

Incidentally, the 600 was not only large, beautifully engineered, and sumptuously furnished, but it was also very fast. Even the seven-seater Pullman could be urged up to speeds in excess of 120mph (193km/h), and the acceleration was something of which many a sports car would have been proud. The fuel consumption, admittedly, could be rather horrifying, but, to bowdlerize a famous saying: "If you have to ask the price, you can't afford it."

Many respected motoring writers, having driven the 600, thought that it handled like a sports car. When they came to drive the 230SL, which had been announced a few months earlier, they knew it *was* a sports car through and through. But sports-car standards had changed a lot since the heroic days of the Porsche-designed SSK monsters, or even in the short time since the 300SL had been launched. The 230SL was certainly not a noisy-exhaust-and-wind-through-the-hair car, but a thoroughly modern machine. For although the 230SL was certainly fast and was possessed of very good road manners, it was also very completely equipped and—in the optional hardtop form—it had all the refinement and snug comfort of a compact little sedan car.

What made the 230SL so distinctive and so readily recognized by anyone with even the vaguest interest in motoring was its styling. In open roadster guise, perhaps, its sleek lines were perhaps no more than one might have expected from a Mercedes-Benz of the period, but the lines of the optional hardtop were unique, and never copied by any other manufacturer. The reason was simple—on almost every car ever designed up to that time, the roof panel was shaped to fall away gently towards the sides and the junction with the door aperture, but on the 230SL the process was reversed. The lowest point of the roof cross section was in the middle of the car, and the profile actually rose gently towards the cant rails. It needed only one observer to name this a "pagoda roof" and the name stuck. The reason for this profile was interesting, and more significant than it appeared at first. It was done, not for styling effect, but to ease entry into the cockpit. The passenger doors could be higher than usual, and there could be a little more headroom for the passengers.

It certainly made an extra talking point about what was otherwise a rather conventional (by Daimler-Benz standards) sports car. The 230SL was brought in to replace both the 300SL and the 190SL models, and, in truth, was much more like the 190SL in its engineering. That car had evolved from the underpan of the 180 sedan, while the 230SL evolved from the underpan and mechanical components of the 220SE sedan, though it used an engine which had been enlarged from 133.9 to 140.7cu in (2195 to 2306cc) with a slightly increased cylinder bore, and was considerably more powerful with a peak output of 150bhp (DIN).

It had not, of course, been possible to provide a direct replacement for the 300SL Roadster (but what car, after all, could ever have done that?), so Daimler-Benz had to expect some criticism of the 230SL's performance at first. Perhaps, on reflection, the press were less than fair to the 230SLs, which could reach a maximum speed of more than 120mph (193km/h), without strain and without disturbing the composure of the passengers. Certainly there was no complaint from the customers, who flocked to buy these smart little two-seaters in considerable numbers. More than 8000 cars were built in 1969 — six years after the model was first seen — and total production in rather less than eight years approached 50,000.

Even within months of the 230SL being announced, however, Daimler-Benz had proved that the 230SL was more, much more, than a pretty "boulevard" sports car. They entered a factory-prepared car for "works" rally driver Eugen Bohringer to use in the grueling Liège–Sofia–Liège marathon and on this, its maiden event, it won outright, and showed great reliability and strength.

Unlike the 600 model, which was still essentially the same in the mid-1970s as it had been when launched in 1963, the 230SL received regular attention from engineers and product planners. For 1967 the 230SL was re-engined with the 152.2cu in (2496cc) modified 250SE engine, which produced much more torque but no more peak power, and was given four-wheel disk brakes, thus becoming the 250SL. Only a year later, at the beginning of 1968, the 250SL became the 280SL, mainly because the latest 169.5cu in (2778cc) overhead cam-shaft six-cylinder engine (which peaked at 170bhp) took over as the standard power plant. The 280SL, in fact, was the most popular derivative of this family of cars, and was still selling strongly when it was eventually phased out early in 1971 in favor of the much bulkier, and rather faster, 350SL/450SLC range.

While all this was going on, Daimler-Benz had not been standing back from the improvement of its quantity-production cars. Even though the W111 and W112 models introduced in 1959 had since burgeoned into a large number of sedans, two-door coupes and convertibles, with a whole variety of engines, a start was made in replacing them in 1965. As usual with Daimler-Benz in recent years, it was not a clean-cut change from one car to the next. The last of the *original* unit-construction sedans (whose pedigree dated from 1953) disappeared, and *some* of the 1959 vintage were also phased out. Remaining derivatives were shuffled round, and the first of a new family (the W108/W109 models) were brought in. In the process, Daimler-Benz moved progressively up-market, as the smallest of its current cars now weighed 2800lb (1270kg) and had a 122.0cu in (2.0-liter) engine.

The new cars abandoned the finned style of their predecessors, used a long horizontal design, and were less flamboyant and less assertive than the obsolescent machines. There was more glass, and lower front and rear lid lines. Engines were revised, enlarged, and made more powerful. Although the 182.8cu in (2996cc) engine made famous by the 300SL was retained for a time in the newly bodied 300SE, a final stretch (to 169.5cu in/2778cc) of the middle-size six-cylinder engine was already in preparation, and it took over in 1968.

These cars, however, went only part of the way towards the standards which Daimler-Benz was investigating for its cars of the 1970s. The change in styling, in market emphasis, and in the standard of furnishing, was already underway, but it was still being done with well-proven mechanical components, and with a few outdated features like the swing-axle rear suspension. The very successful foray into sports-car and Grand Prix racing had already been completed, and a great deal had been done to update the production cars. Now, towards the end of the 1960s, it was time for a "New Generation" of cars to be developed, and in 1968 the first of these fine cars was revealed.

7. POSTWAR MOTORSPORT

In 1945 there was no question of a speedy return to International motor-sport by Daimler-Benz. The obstacles, financial and practical, looked to be insuperable. Not only had the factories been flattened and many records lost, but the surviving racing cars were widely dispersed. Many technicians and mechanics would never return to their peacetime work. This, however, did not stop that most avid racing enthusiast, Alfred Neubauer, from planning ahead.

In 1939 the three distinct types of Mercedes-Benz racing cars—the 1937 347.8cu in (5.7-liter) W125s, the 1938/1939 183.1cu in (3.0-liter) W154s, and the two "Tripoli cars," the 91.5cu in (1.5-liter) W165s—had all been taken to safe places well away from the main factories, and stored in workshops, farm-houses and barns. The idea was good, and would have been justified—except that by May 1945 a high proportion of the cars found themselves as "political prisoners" behind the line of Russian advance. Neubauer, therefore, could not hope to recover every car, and even resorted to barter on one occasion when it was discovered that two W154 racing cars were for sale on a used car lot in Berlin! Rudi Caracciola, in the meantime, had already managed to spirit the 91.5cu in (1.5-liter) W165s out of Germany into Switzerland, where they were promptly seized by the Swiss authorities.

For a while, in any case, the Grand Prix scene was in turmoil, but a new racing formula eventually emerged, in which eligible cars could use 274.6cu in (4.5-liter) unsupercharged engines, or 91.5cu in (1.5-liter) supercharged units. If only the W165s could have been freed, and if only political and financial conditions had been right, they could have been ideal contenders for this new formula. But it was not to be—another prewar model, the Alfa Romeo Alfetta, took advantage of its state of readiness, and dominated the sport for several years.

Analysis showed that there was really no place for the big W125 models in postwar motor racing, so the remaining cars were consigned to the museum at Stuttgart. On very special occasions, even more than 40 years after they were last raced, they are fired up once again and demonstrated in public. One further car, which Neubauer thought had disappeared forever, was discovered in Eastern Europe by a British enthusiast, purchased, rebuilt, and was raced in "historic" events in Britain and Europe, before being resold to a collector.

The remarkable little W165s, too, were never used again. The Swiss authorities finally sold them off in 1950; the highest bid came from the Swiss Mercedes-Benz importers, who promptly returned them to Stuttgart. Although there was a tentative proposal to reprepare the 1939 cars for Grand Prix racing in 1951, and even for five completely new cars to be manufactured, the idea was rescinded after the technicians had observed the pace of modern Grand Prix cars. They were lucky, too, for the formula under which the cars would have raced was dying on its feet; after the Alfa-Romeo-versus-Ferrari battle of 1951, Alfa withdrew from the sport, and for the next couple of years Formula One was in abeyance.

The W154 cars, however, were seen again in factory and in private hands. The private entry came from Tommy Lee in North America, who purchased a bedraggled old W154 which had been "found" in Czechoslovakia immediately after the war, and resold to him through a British intermediary. It was entered for the Indianapolis 500 race in 1947 and 1948, but suffered an engine failure in the first year and cooling problems on its second appearance.

By 1950, however, Daimler-Benz was fast returning to economic health, and refurnished W154s were tested in preparation for entry in the 1951 season. Three cars, driven by Juan-Manuel Fangio, Karl Kling and Hermann Lang, entered two races at Buenos Aires in February, but were beaten on both

Previous page: The Eifelrennen in May 1955 was dominated by the 300SLRs. Leading here is Karl Kling, with Fangio second and Stirling Moss third. Fangio actually won the race.

Right: Two prototype "gull-wing" 300SLs started Le Mans in 1952 and two finished – in first and second places.

occasions by Froilan Gonzales in an up-to-date supercharged 122.0cu in (2.0-liter) Ferrari. Lang and Fangio were second and third on the first occasion, Kling and Lang on the second occasion. It was sad, but true, that the cars were no longer completely competitive, and, since Daimler-Benz were, above all things, not interested in being graceful losers, a projected official entry in the 1951 Indianapolis 500 was canceled.

On the Monday following the German Grand Prix where Daimler-Benz top management had seen Ascari's 274.6cu in (4.5-liter) Ferrari defeat the combined might of Alfa-Romeo, Fritz Nallinger held a meeting to discuss the company's racing future. It was a momentous day. It was decided not only that the W154s should be retired, but that three entirely new competition cars should be developed—a sports car for the 1952 season, a Grand Prix car for the new 152.6cu in (2.5-liter) formula, and a sports racing car to be developed from the Grand Prix car's engineering. The 1952 car should use many standard production parts, and the others could be entirely special.

The 300SLR two-seaters led every race which they contested, but were withdrawn from Le Mans after the horrifying accident. This was the start of Eifelrennen in May 1955, with the three factory cars already pulling away from the field. Left to right: Juan Manuel Fangio (the eventual winner), Stirling Moss and Karl Kling.

Nallinger and Uhlenhaut had been greatly impressed with the Jaguar XK120C's winning performance at Le Mans in 1951, with a special body/chassis design housing modified XK120 mechanical components, and speedily decided that they could do the same using their new postwar Type 300 sedan as a starting point. The sensational 300SL was the result.

Developed in the first place as a racing sports car, but eventually put into quantity production as a road car of the "Supercar" variety, the 300SL broke new ground, not only in its mechanical design, but also in its body engineering. Every mechanical element of the new 1951 sedan, the 300, went into the new racing sports car—engine, gearbox, rear axle and suspensions—but all were thoroughly re-worked for their new purpose. The chassis of the new car, coded W194, however, was unique and startling in its conception. It was the first automotive application of that aviation-derived concept, the multi-tube space frame.

A true space frame is a three-dimensional complex of small diameter tubes linking all the major stress and dead loading points; each tube is only subjected to tension or compression forces, but must never be required to withstand bending or torsion. In a two-seater car, where access has to be provided for passengers and their means of exit and ingress—not forgetting the space which must be provided for the bulky engine—practicality is always in conflict with the theoretical ideal.

In the new car, the 300SL, the major problem was to provide chassis beam strength, which could only be ensured by having high-sided chassis rails. To allow passenger access to the cockpit, very high door sills were needed, and as the engineers did not want to hang the doors from the windshield pillar this almost automatically forced them to use top-hinged doors in a fixed coupe roof. Thus, by default as much as by intention, Mercedes-Benz engineers invented the famous "gull-wing" door layout of the 300SL.

In 1952, however, there were three different types of racing 300SL. The original cars had very shallow doors comprising only the side windows and part of the roof panels, but for Le Mans the doors were deepened, with openings stretching further down the body sides. Later in the year, some of the cars were converted for use on open roads, with tiny front-hinged doors.

To minimize the height of the cars and to optimize the wind-cheating properties of the body style, the bulky six-cylinder engine was canted over 50 degrees towards the left side of the chassis. On all the racing 300SLs, fuel supply was by means of carburetors, though when the production car appeared in 1954 it was equipped with an early form of Bosch fuel injection, with the nozzles supplying fuel direct to the combustion chambers.

The 300SL's first race entry was only partially successful—with Kling and Caracciola finishing second and fourth in the Mille Miglia—but thereafter there was no mistake. A 1-2-3 finish was achieved in the Bern sports car race, a 1-2 finish at Le Mans (with Hermann Lang and Fritz Riess winning after Levegh's Talbot-Lago had failed at a late stage), an easy win at the Nurburgring, and an astonishing and unexpected 1-2 victory in the grueling Carrera Panamericana road race in Mexico. During the season the engines were supercharged on occasion, and for Mexico they were enlarged to 189.2cu in (3.1-liters). However,

Speedy roadside service for one of the "gull-wing" 300SLs, which was competing in the long-distance open-road Carrera Panamericana race of 1952.

although a 1953 program was originally proposed in which many new features (including low-pivot swing-axle rear suspension) were to have been proved, this was the last works-sponsored appearance of the 300SLs, as all efforts were henceforth concentrated on the new Grand Prix cars.

It is worth noting that the production 300SL was on sale from 1954 to 1963; the "gull-wing" coupe gave way to the more conventionally styled roadster in 1957. A total of 3258 300SLs were sold, of which 1400 were "gull-wings" (and 29 of them had special light-alloy bodies). These "gull-wings" of course, are now highly-prized collectors' items.

The 300SL racing program, even though highly successful, was never meant to be more than an intensive prelude to greater things. In it the engineers discovered that the opposition was by no means as fearsome as they had expected, and in particular that professionalism was often lacking. More than any other car, Daimler-Benz had feared the Jaguar XK120C at Le Mans in 1952—in the event, it was found that Jaguar feared the 300SL, had made panic changes to their body shapes and cooling systems, and suffered the ignominy of early retirement with engine failures caused by faulty and untested cooling. . . .

No one at Stuttgart and, it seemed, no one elsewhere in the world of motor racing expected the new Grand Prix cars to fail, and they were not to be disappointed. It is only fair to point out, however, that very few racing cars have ever spent more than two years being developed and tested before they were first raced, and none was backed by the expertise of an organization like that of Daimler-Benz.

The new W196 Grand Prix car (and here, from time to time, I must cross-refer to its close design relative, the W196S sports-racing car, more generally

During the 1952 Carrera Panamericana, held in Mexico, steel bars were fitted across the screens of the 300SLs to protect the windshield from damage by animals (or large flying stones). Kling and Klenk drove this car to outright victory at more than 102mph (163km/h).

known as the 300SLR), sketched out in 1952, designed and developed in 1953, built, tested and first raced in 1954, dominated the Grand Prix scene from the day that it raced at Rheims in July 1954 until its last race in the fall of 1955. No other racing car has ever burst into the Grand Prix scene in such a completely successful manner. In less than 18 months, W196 cars won 11 major races, including nine *Grande Epreuves*; of more importance, they were only defeated on three occasions, and they helped that remarkable Argentinian driver, Juan-Manuel Fangio, to win two successive World Championships.

The W196, while similar in design philosophy to the earlier 300SL, was entirely different in detail. Its space-frame chassis was wrapped round a new eight-cylinder 152.6cu in (2.5-liter) engine which was tipped sharply to the right, the five-speed gearbox was at the rear in unit with the differential, there was a low-pivot swing-axle rear suspension, and the huge finned drum brakes were inboard at front and rear. It was not officially admitted for some time, but the layout was also conducive to the eventual adoption of four-wheel-drive as development progressed.

The most startling feature of the original 1954 car was that it was equipped with a full-width, streamlined, sports-car style body, in which the wheels were enclosed, although the driver was centrally placed. This body shape was intended for use on high-speed circuits like Rheims and Monza, but a more conventional open-wheel alternative was also to be provided for most other circuits.

The engine itself was startling enough, even without the distractions of the chassis engineering. Grand Prix "straight eights" were, in any case, rare enough in modern times, but those built from a clever (and traditional Daimler-Benz) mixture of castings and sheet steel fabrications were unique. In addition the crankshaft had roller bearings, the cylinder head had "down-draft" inlet ports, and there was direct fuel injection through cylinder walls. The most astonishing feature, however, and one which has never successfully been used on any other engine, was the desmodromic valve gear, in which the valves were positively opened *and* closed by cams. All in all, it was an immensely complex racing engine which no less-well-equipped concern could ever have tackled. At the beginning of its racing life in 1954 it disposed of 257bhp at 8250rpm, and by the end of 1955 this had been raised to 290bhp at 8500rpm; reliability was astonishingly high.

In the short Grand Prix program these statistics tell their story: 42 cars started in 13 World Championship events, of which 27 finished, and nine wins were achieved. However, the story is not purely confined to the dominance of one particular type of car, but to the versatility and dedication of the 200 engineers, designers and mechanics, backed up by the 300 skilled toolmakers, who tailored cars to each particular event. There were only two debacles: first, in the cars' second race, the British Grand Prix at Silverstone in 1954, where Fangio's car was handicapped by poor handling and traction, and the difficulties of vision from the cockpit of the fully streamlined body shell which had never really been intended for this tight type of circuit; and second, in the 1955 Monaco Grand Prix where every W196 retired from the event.

By the end of the 1955 season, not only had the cars been raced in fully streamlined and in open-wheeler guise, but they had been built in original (long), medium, and short wheelbase form, some with the all-inboard braking layout and some with outboard front brakes. Generally speaking, streamlined cars were only built on the long-wheelbase chassis, but for Monza in 1955 a pair of experimental medium-wheelbase streamliners were prepared. It is a measure of the company's resources that, when these cars were found to be unsatisfactory, one spare long-wheelbase car was prepared for Fangio to drive,

Juan Manuel Fangio, the acknowledged Mercedes-Benz team leader in 1955, practices for the British Grand Prix at the Aintree Circuit in the shortest-chassis derivative of the phenomenal W196 design. He finished second in the race, just a car's length behind Stirling Moss's sister car.

The start of a truly epic drive in the 1955 Mille Miglia by Stirling Moss and Denis Jenkinson. Their 300SLR pulverized the record for the event, and now stands for all time. Fangio's car, driven alone, was second, many minutes behind the British pair.

Below: This 1955 300SLR is "numbered up" as Stirling Moss's Mille Miglia winning car, but it is not, for that car had twin headrests and an uncovered passenger seat. Even Daimler-Benz, it seems, is not above bending the absolute truth for publicity purposes.

Left: Detail of the 1955 two-seater 300SLR sports racing car shows the metal cover usually carried over the passenger seat and the simple instrument panel.

and a new long-wheelbase car was assembled *in two days* at Stuttgart (from existing parts) for Moss to drive.

The first appearance of the W196 Grand Prix cars, in the French Grand Prix at Rheims in July 1954, fulfilled all the hopes of Daimler-Benz management. Four cars arrived at the circuit, three raced, two started from the front row of the grid, and two finished first and second in the race, driven by Fangio and Kling. All Rheims lap records were smashed, and the opposition was pulverized. The press immediately dubbed these cars the Silver Arrows, a name which stuck—it was almost as if they had never been away.

In the next 18 months, there was rarely a problem in making the cars competitive, but there was often some difficulty in achieving Mercedes-Benz standards of reliability. There was no doubt not only that the cars were somewhat bulky and therefore heavy in their use of fuel, but that their handling was sometimes suspect, and that they needed better brakes. There was no way of making major handling improvements, as this was limited by the policy decision to use swing-axle rear suspension and Continental tires, but it seems strange that the engineers at Stuttgart stayed faithful to drum brakes when some of their rivals (notably Jaguar) had proved that disk brakes were much superior.

Even so, their overall performance was good enough to ensure World Championships in each season. Of seven races entered in 1954, the cars won in

1954 Type W196 Grand Prix Car

Engine: Eight cylinders, in line, in nine-bearing steel-cylinder block with separate light-alloy crankcase, installed in car at an angle of 70 degrees. Bore and stroke, capacity: 2.99×2.71in, 152.3cu in (76×68.8mm, 2496cc). Nondetachable steel cylinder head in unit with block. Two overhead valves per cylinder, opposed at 88 degrees, operated by twin overhead camshafts, and desmodromic (ie, positive opening and closing of valves) valve gear. Dry sump lubrication. Bosch direct fuel injection. Maximum power: 280bhp at 8500rpm.

Transmission: Single-dry-plate clutch in unit with front-mounted engine. Open propeller shaft to five-speed synchromesh manual gearbox (no synchromesh on first gear) in unit with chassis-mounted spiral bevel final drive. Remote-control right-hand gearchange. Exposed, universally jointed drive shafts to rear wheels.

Chassis: Separate multi-tubular space frame with many small-diameter steel tubes linking points of stress. Light alloy single-seater body shell in two styles – fully enveloping or exposed wheels. Independent front suspension by longitudinal torsion bars and wishbones. Independent rear suspension by low-pivot swing axles, Watts linkage location, and torsion bars. Telescopic dampers. Steering wheel removable for access to seat.

Steering by worm and sector. Four-wheel hydraulically operated drum brakes, inboard at front and rear. Center-lock 16in wire wheels. Front tires: 6.00×16in, rear tires: 7.00×16in.

Dimensions: Wheelbase 7ft 8.5in (2.35m). Front track: 4ft 4.5in (1.33m), rear track: 4ft 5in (1.35m). Overall length not quoted. Unladen weight (streamlined version): 1540lb (698kg).

*The W196 Grand Prix car's maiden appearance,
at Rheims in the French Grand Prix of July
1954, was in long-wheelbase streamlined form.
Juan Manuel Fangio (car 18) won the race,
and Karl Kling (No 20) finished second. No
better debut could have been planned.*

Right: The start of the 1955 British Grand Prix at Aintree near Liverpool with Fangio's and Moss's shortest-wheelbase W196 models in the front row, and with Taruffi (No 50) and Karl Kling behind them. Maserati No 2 was driven by Jean Behra.

Above: Story without words – a signed souvenir picture of the victorious Daimler-Benz team after the 1955 British Grand Prix. The drivers along with Uhlenhaut and Neubauer are grouped around one of the Austin-Healeys used to parade them around the track before the start.

France, Germany, Switzerland, Italy and (in a non-championship event) at the Avus track in Berlin, and lost in Britain due to handling problems, and in Spain due to poor brakes and overheating engines. In 1955, when the full range of derivatives became available, there were wins in Argentina [twice—one being a non-championship event in which 183.1cu in (3.0-liter) 300SLR engines were used], Belgium, Holland, Britain and Italy. There were no finishers in the European Grand Prix round the Monaco circuit, when all three cars retired with the same engine problem.

In 1955, indeed, the performance of the silver cars was so superior that rigid team orders were invariably issued—that Fangio was to win wherever possible, and that Stirling Moss, who had joined the team in 1955, should finish second. There were three such finishes, though in Britain it was Moss who was allowed to win his "home" race by just a length from the Argentinian master. In that race, incidentally, Daimler-Benz entered four open-wheel cars and finished in first, second, third and fourth positions.

While all this was going on (and it now seems incredible that this should ever have been possible) the company was also heavily and completely successfully involved in World Championship sports-car racing. Admittedly they were not ready to race in 1954, but in the 1955 season several 300SLR two-seaters were entered in six races, won five of them, and were withdrawn from the sixth race when leading it. But if Fangio was the master of the Grand Prix cars, Stirling Moss was the great virtuoso in the 300SLRs; he won three of the races—the difficult three—and finished second, immediately behind Fangio, in the other races.

None of this would have been possible, one suspects, if the 300SLRs had not been so like the W196 Grand Prix cars in so many ways. In general layout they were the same, but for obvious reasons there were some differences: to accommodate two passengers there was a wider space-frame chassis; the streamlined open body shell had different lines and was fitted with headlights and other necessary equipment; the straight-eight cylinder engine had a one-piece light-alloy block casting, a cast head in place of the hybrid cast/pressed units used in the single-seaters, and it was also enlarged to 183.1cu in (3.0-liter) capacity. In 1954 test form the engine produced more than 280bhp, but the actual 1955 racing 300SLRs had more than 300bhp at 7500rpm.

Although entries were made for the 300SLR to compete at Le Mans in 1954, this was premature, and the first public appearance of the car was in testing at Monza in September 1954. Its first race, the 1955 Mille Miglia on public roads in Italy, was completely successful, for Stirling Moss (partnered by Denis Jenkinson, of *Motor Sport* magazine) won at a record average speed of 97.7mph (157.2km/h), and his team-mate Fangio (driving alone) finished second. Moss's performance, aided by his undoubted genius and the performance of the 300SLR, was further helped by meticulous practice and the innovative navigation of co-driver Jenkinson. It is a Mille Miglia record which now stands for all time.

Apart from two relatively unimportant (in sporting terms) wins in Germany and Sweden, the 300SLRs were also rewarded with other major victories in the British Tourist Trophy (by Moss and his co-driver John Fitch) and in the Sicilian Targa Florio (by Moss and Peter Collins), but their greatest disappointment, and a major tragedy, occurred at Le Mans. In that event, the cars had been equipped with revolutionary new air brakes, which could be raised by the drivers and which, when folded, were effectively a double body skin on the tail. For two hours after the start of this 24-hour event, a furious battle developed for the lead between Fangio's 300SLR, Mike Hawthorn's Jaguar D-Type and Castelotti's Ferrari, with Levegh's 300SLR not far behind. An unfortunate chain of events led to too many ultra-fast cars converging on the narrow pits area at the same time, and the tragic result was that the Frenchman's 300SLR was catapulted into the grandstand where it exploded killing more than 80 spectators and Levegh himself.

It took hours for Daimler-Benz management to react to this shock, during which time the surviving 300SLRs of Moss/Fangio and Kling/Simon consolidated their position. Before half-distance in this 24-hour race, however, Neubauer was instructed to withdraw the cars, as a mark of respect to the dead in the tragedy, and two healthy 300SLRs were silently wheeled away. It was no consolation to anyone that the Moss/Fangio car held a two lap lead over Mike Hawthorn's D-Type Jaguar at that point.

Within days of the Le Mans tragedy, Daimler-Benz directors had met to consider their company's future policy towards motorsport. On the one hand there was grief and real distress at the Le Mans tragedy, while on the other there was the definite knowledge that they were already supreme in both types of racing, and could prove nothing more. There and then it was decided that they should withdraw from Grand Prix racing at the end of the year, but that the 300SLR program should continue; even that withdrawal was extended, immediately after the Targa Florio victory, when it was decided even to

Fangio at the end of one of his most grueling drives. He won the 1955 Argentine Grand Prix (his home ground) in a medium-wheelbase W196.

Above: If the driver of a big Mercedes-Benz sedan was determined enough, he could be very fast indeed on loose surfaces. Andrew Cowan (280E) in the 1977 London–Sydney rally which he won.

Below: Even though Andrew Cowan's 280E was driven almost flat out for more than 15,000 miles (24,000km) in the 1977 London–Sydney rally, it was almost completely reliable. A sister car (driven by Tony Fowkes) was second.

withdraw completely and totally from sports-car racing.

The might-have-beens are even more interesting than the actual successes. How fast would the four-wheel-drive W196 single-seater have been, and would it have struck as much roadholding trouble as the later breed of single seaters did at the end of the 1960s? Would either of the two coupe 300SLRs built, but never raced, have been as sensationally fast as they promised to be? What might the performance of either car have been with all the technical developments already underway for 1956? Or with the disk brakes, which must surely have been adopted before long? No one knew and no one ever found out, for the management kept its promise and never sold off any of the redundant machines; of the 15 Grand Prix W196s and the ten 300SLRs, all were either preserved at Stuttgart, or were sent out on extended loan or as greatly appreciated gifts, to motoring collections or museums all over the world. Better yet, examples of each are still kept in running order and appear in demonstrations on the race tracks of the world.

At the end of 1955 the shut down was almost complete. The staff was dispersed and many of the designers returned to the no less vital task of designing new production cars. Alfred Neubauer also left the racing scene, but turned his attention to the museum at Stuttgart, particularly to the upkeep of the many famous racing and record cars in the collection. Neubauer, a man both physically and in reputation considerably larger than life, eventually became a consultant to Daimler-Benz, and died in 1980, at the age of 89.

A nucleus of competition activity was, however, maintained at Daimler-Benz, originally under Karl Kling, and later under Baron von Korff, where the accent was mainly on rallying and very occasional forays into touring-car racing. Walter Schock became European Touring Car Champion in the rallies of 1956 and again in 1960 (a year remembered for that magnificently planned 1-2-3 victory in the Monte Carlo Rally, when Mercedes-Benz virtually invented the idea of a month-long practice for this major event). Schock was then supplanted by the diminutive Eugen Bohringer, who in combination with the rugged and fast 220SE and 300SE sedans was virtually unbeatable in rough-road events. Bohringer, a restauranteur from Stuttgart, was European champion in 1962, and in 1963 established the remarkable precedent of winning the very grueling Liège–Sofia–Liège marathon with a 230SL coupe in its very first motoring event.

By this time, too, Juan-Manuel Fangio had become the importer of Mercedes-Benz models into Argentina, and persuaded the factory regularly to send cars to compete in the Argentine Road Race, which was run mainly on unsurfaced tracks in the outback and the Andes. Walter Schock won in 1961, which was fairly predictable, but in 1962 the event was won outright by the beautiful Swedish girl Ewy Rosqvist, who was clearly so attracted by the Daimler-Benz approach to motoring that she eventually became Baroness von Korff. Eugen Bohringer won the event again in 1963 and 1964, after which there seemed to be no point in proving the same supremacy time and time again.

By the end of the 1960s the chain of experience, of know-how, and of success, linked with the 1950s, was becoming very fragile, and in retrospect it is easy to see why Daimler-Benz found it so demanding to get a serious competition program underway once again. The mid-engined C111 sports prototype,

with its three-rotor or even four-rotor Wankel engine, was potentially as good a racing car as anything then being built by Porsche or Ferrari, but in the absence of a racing formula which properly took account of the Wankel engine there was no way that Daimler-Benz could prove it. Similarly, any attempt to get back into production sedan-car racing [even with a 384.4cu in (6.3-liter) engined 300SEL] was doomed by the lack of commitment to homologation of special parts, and to a concerted program.

The link between the 1960s and the late 1970s, however, was a burly development engineer called Erich Waxenberger, who won the Macao six-hour touring car race in a 384.4cu in. (6.3-liter) engined car, and who has been the guiding genius behind the rallying program which evolved gradually but inexorably in the late 1970s.

Sensing, as have other sizeable concerns in the European motor industry, that the customers are equally as impressed by rallying victories with quantity-production cars as they are by racing victories in prototypes, Daimler-Benz decided to get back into rallying, initially by stealth. After seeing that its standard products, prepared (and paid for) at the request of private owners, could perform with credit in the rougher, long-distance, rallies of the world, the firm really got back into the sport by building a fleet of strengthened but otherwise standard 280E sedans for the 1977 London–Sydney Marathon. Andrew Cowan made it all worthwhile by winning the event outright in a 280E, while his Mercedes-Benz "rival" Tony Fowkes finished second.

A year later it was time to get more serious, for more "private" entries appeared in the East African Safari, but suffered from inexperience in local conditions, and only Zasada's car survived to finish sixth. In South America, however, in August and September, for the 30,000km (18,645-mile) Vuelta a la America del Sud, there was no mistake. Waxenberger supplied a fleet of 450SLC coupes and 280E sedans to highly paid drivers, who duly rewarded him by dominating an incredibly long event, and collecting the first five places, with Andrew Cowan and Sobieslaw Zasada in first and second places in 450SLCs and Tony Fowkes third in a 280E.

Two major outings in 1979 were the Safari once again, where the 305.1cu in (5.0-liter) engined 450SLCs might have won if it had not been for mechanical misfortune (yet Hannu Mikkola managed to finish second), and in Bandama where no fewer than four 450SLC 5.0s driven respectively by Mikkola, Bjorn Waldegard, Andrew Cowan and Vic (Junior) Preston, took the first four places. It seemed that the big coupes were ideal in rough and loose going, and a full World Championship program was planned for 1980.

At this point, however, it became clear that basically standard cars, even if as well-engineered as the latest 500SLCs were, could not usually beat the very special rallying machines from other concerns. Throughout the 1980 season the 500SLCs were dogged by misfortune and mechanical failures, and only managed to notch up a single outright victory. That, however, is precisely the sort of failure which Daimler-Benz will not tolerate, and we may be sure that better and more concentrated efforts are planned for the 1980s.

On the other hand, it is not likely that a return will be made to the Grand Prix racing scene—not, that is, until the accent swings firmly away from the present "Show Business" type of racing, and back to the sort of racing which attracted major manufacturers in the 1930s, 1940s and 1950s. Aggravation over regulations, sponsorship, and high finance is something which Daimler-Benz can do without. One thing, of course, is absolutely certain—that if a return *is* made, it will be a full-blooded attack, with cars which should be capable of winning. That, at least, is a prospect which will intrigue Mercedes-Benz lovers for some years to come.

8. MODERN TIMES—WORLD LEADERS

Twenty years ago, if you had asked anyone, anywhere, the identity of the world's best car, the answer would have been immediate — Rolls-Royce. To pose the question at the beginning of the 1980s would bring a divided response — those who did not know, and had not driven either, would still say "Rolls-Royce," but those wealthy enough, and percipient enough, to have found out for themselves, might say "Mercedes-Benz." By the 1970s, indeed, Daimler-Benz had firmly established itself on its pinnacle; it was by Daimler-Benz standards that every other passenger car in the world was matched.

The suspicion that they *might* be able to build the world's finest cars had been lurking around the corridors of Daimler-Benz's top management for some years, but it was not until the 1960s, when the vast and prestigious 600 Limousine had successfully been launched, that the firm knew that it *could* build the best. Perhaps, as a first attempt, the 600 was not yet the best, but by producing the car the company had breached technological and philosophical barriers. Before the 600 appeared, there might have been a touch of self-doubt and envy — of the reputation and traditions of Rolls-Royce or of the resources of Cadillac, perhaps — now there was none.

By the mid-1960s, twenty years after the rebuilding of the shattered factories had begun, all practical, physical and financial constraints had been shrugged off. A series of major model introductions in the 1950s and early 1960s had presented Daimler-Benz with a high and still-growing reputation, an enviable spread of market penetration, and a truly comprehensive series of component "building blocks" with which to juggle its future. Sales had been rising steadily year after year, and before long annual production would reach the quarter-million mark for the very first time.

Already, at Sindelfingen, a settled pattern of passenger-car production was evident. Two distinctly different types of normal touring car were being built in a complex series of subtly different models and body styles, along with the sleek and self-indulgent 230SL coupes and convertibles, and the limited-production 600 Limousines and Pullmans. The smaller and — by definition — cheaper touring cars were only built as sedans and fixed-head coupes, but the larger touring cars were available as sedans, coupes and convertibles.

In terms of numbers built, incidentally, the 600 models were something of an irrelevance, even (if only anyone dared to admit it) something of a disruptive nuisance, but their worth in marketing and publicity terms made all the aggravation seem worthwhile.

This, therefore, is a pattern which has not changed significantly in the last 15 years, and indeed is one which carries on into the 1980s. It is, of course, quite true that Daimler-Benz offerings for the early 1980s are mostly very different from those of the 1960s, but they still cover the same market, with the same enormously complex interlock of optional engines, transmissions, wheelbases and equipment. The 600, however, which has never been a large-scale production proposition, is now hand built. Times, fashions — and safety regulations — have, however, changed the model mix. Almost all the convertibles have gone and, for the first time ever on a factory-built basis, there are station wagons in the range.

In the period covered by this chapter — which is effectively the mid-1960s to the early 1980s — there have been many new models, and a myriad of subtle but commercially important improvements. Yet there has never been a time when change came as a shock, or cars produced which were visually very different from those they replaced. In some cases (for example, when the new "S" class cars for the 1980s replaced the original 1972–1979 variety at the Frankfurt motor show) it was often difficult to accept that a new body shell was actually

Previous page: The latest range of S-class sedan cars for the 1980s – 280SE, 380SE and 500SE versions. All share the same body sheet metal.

involved. In styling, more than in any other aspect of design and engineering, Daimler-Benz managers obviously believe in continuity.

It has been a period in which every model range has been completely changed at least once, and in most cases twice, well before the public had tired of the existing cars. No fewer than four entirely different new engine ranges have been introduced, and several significant changes to existing ranges have also appeared. There was also time to produce new automatic transmissions and manual gearboxes — Daimler-Benz, incidentally, is among the exclusive group of car makers who find it worthwhile to build their own automatics, rather than buy them in from proprietary concerns. The first move was made, in 1979, into what I will rather sweepingly call the "Range Rover/Jeep four-wheel-drive" market.

It has been a period of steady but quite remarkably consistent expansion, in which existing factories have been improved and persistently re-equipped, and

The Daimler-Benz sporting cars of the 1970s were supplied in short-wheelbase two-seater or longer-wheelbase four-seater forms. This is the four-seater 350SLC version.

The second of the S-class models was that built, with great and lasting success, between 1972 and 1980. This particular car was a 1979 450SEL derivative; it was fitted with the 4in longer wheelbase (L = Long, in most languages), and it had the 4.5-liter (274.6cu in) V8 engine option.

in which major new facilities (like the ex-Borgward factory at Bremen, and a new venture with Steyr-Daimler-Puch at Graz in Austria) have been established. In 1980, even before the much-rumored "small Mercedes-Benz" models made their appearance, there were at least 40 distinctly different models in the range. Sales in the 1970s grew inexorably from 280,000 units in 1970 to 422,000 in 1979. Daimler-Benz even managed to increase its output between 1973 and 1974, a time when almost every manufacturer of cars in the Western world was sent reeling by the shock of the oil crisis, and the huge price increases which speedily followed.

It would need a complete, separate, and very complex book even to write down and explain the nuances and the development of Daimler-Benz model policy in recent years, so it follows that the author can only hope to trace the major changes, milestones and achievements, at the same time as he mentions the most fascinating, and infuriatingly unavailable, Mercedes of all, the C111 coupe. One thing, however, is no longer in doubt—there are now many discerning customers ready to swear that Daimler-Benz can build the best cars in the world; in many cases the company's own impeccable standards have to be trimmed with an eye to costs, but in the case of magnificent flagships like the 450SEL 6.9 there are no excuses to be made. The fact that a Rolls-Royce Silver Shadow, or Silver Spirit, might be more exclusive, or that a Cadillac sells in much bigger quantities, is not important. In engineering, quality, and durability terms, a top-of-the-line Mercedes-Benz model stands supreme.

Although the great surge forward to modern times began at Daimler-Benz with the announcement of the "New Generation" models of 1968, the new

After use as Wankel-engined test cars, the C111 mid-engined prototypes turned to other tasks. This example was given a turbocharged five-cylinder diesel engine producing about 190bhp, and used to set several international speed records.

atmosphere and the new confidence of the engineers is better signified by the incredible C111 coupes which were first shown in 1969. Not only did these cars prove that Daimler-Benz engineers had never lost touch with modern motor racing, but that they were, as ever, likely to do a better job with new concepts and new technology than any other team. For not only was the C111 an ultramodern mid-engined two-seater coupe, but it was powered by a Wankel engine!

Quietly, and without fuss, Daimler-Benz had agreed to a license to develop its own Wankel rotary engine in the early 1960s, but of course had been upstaged in terms of worldwide publicity by NSU, who put the little Spider on sale in 1963, and the Ro80 sedan in 1967. A design study for a mid-engined Mercedes-Benz car had been made in 1964 before Fritz Nallinger retired from the scene, but it was not until late 1968 that the project was reborn in earnest.

In its mid-engined layout, in its suspension engineering and in its styling, the C111 was altogether typical of the latest racing sports cars, with its pronounced low-nose wedge style and two-seater closed coupe passenger cabin. It had suspension geometry and wheel/tire sizes infinitely more suited to race-track use than to regular open-road motoring in traffic, and in Ing Uhlenhaut's hands it was also set up to handle as well as any latter-day Ferrari, Porsche or Ford GT40. Although Daimler-Benz designers had styled the car themselves, it might equally as well have been shaped by one of the Italian masters, for there are very few ways in which a low-nose high-tail mid-engined coupe can evolve.

The car was revealed, after a short period of delicious rumor had been allowed to spread abroad, in the late summer of 1969. All that was exciting enough, but the real sensation was caused by the engine, which was nothing

less than a triple-rotor Wankel engine, equivalent in size to a 219.7cu in (3.6-liter) piston engine, and rated at no less than 280bhp at 7000rpm. Although it was by no means the first Wankel engine which Daimler-Benz had developed (the first car-type engine had run in 1966), it was the first to be seen in public and, predictably enough, it caused a sensation. It was the first automotive-type Wankel engine to be revealed with three rotors (both the NSU and the Mazda units had twin rotors), and it was much the most powerful of all.

The motoring press was somewhat puzzled by the launch of this car, especially as it was led to understand that only a limited number of the cars *might* be sold in the near future because the C111 was clearly neither a fully-developed and refined road car, nor yet was it a potentially race-winning competition car. There were suggestions, however, that this was merely a case of a forward-looking and prosperous concern's engineering "thinking aloud." This opinion was reinforced at the 1970 Geneva Motor Show when a further derivative of the C111 was shown which had a restyled wedge-shaped body with more window area and better all-around vision, and a stupendously powerful four-rotor Wankel engine rated at no less than 350bhp at 7500rpm, from a nominal 292.9cu in (4.8-liter) capacity unit. The maximum speed of this remarkable research machine was never independently established by one of the important motoring magazines, though Daimler-Benz testers certainly achieved at least 185mph (298km/h). Technical director Rudolf Uhlenhaut obviously found this highly satisfactory, as he adopted a C111 for business and commuting journeys for a time, and (as a surrogate racing driver of no mean standing) was often to be seen traveling at enormous speeds, in great safety, on the motorways in the Stuttgart area.

After that, however, the C111 retired gracefully into the background, and was rarely seen again with a Wankel engine installed. By the early 1970s, indeed, it had become more and more clear that the Wankel concept had not been developed up to an acceptable Daimler-Benz standard of reliability, nor was it proving at all easy to make such units meet the increasingly strict North American anti-emission regulations.

It was not, however, the end of the C111 as a useful chassis, for on several occasions between 1976 and 1979 cars of this type were used to set international speed and endurance records—with a five-cylinder turbocharged diesel engine! This was one of the units evolved for passenger cars in the 1970s, and is described in more detail on a later page. For the C111 installation it was substituted for the multi-rotor Wankel engine, and used in progressively more powerful forms. In 1976, with a boosted output of 190bhp, and with the unmodified C111 body shape retained, the car took a hatful of records in its class up to 5000 miles (8045km), while absolute world records were established at distances of up to 10,000 miles (16,090km). For this purpose, the circular 4.0km (2.5-mile) Nardo proving ground in southern Italy, owned by Fiat, was used, and the very best speed achieved was 156.9mph (252.5km/h) for the first 5000 miles (8045km).

Although this was a truly remarkable demonstration of speed and endurance, and a perfect way of proving to the world that a modern diesel engine could be powerful and sporting as well as a workhorse, it was only a start. Two years later in 1978, with a 230bhp version of the 183.1cu in (3.0-liter) diesel, an aerodynamically modified C111 returned to Nardo to set up nine new absolute world records, including 12 hours at 195.39mph (314.38km/h), and during this run it was found to have a top speed of 202mph (325km/h). By this time, Daimler-Benz was as much interested in testing new synthetic materials and high-speed aerodynamic aids as it was in telling the world about its engines, so in 1979 a radically reshaped C111 went back to Nardo, this time propelled by a

1969 C111 Research Coupe

Engine: Triple-rotor Wankel engine, in light-alloy rotor casing. Displacement of each cylinder, 36.5cu in (600cc), and equivalent "nominal" capacity with piston engine of unit is 219.7cu in (3600cc). Bosch direct-action fuel injection at two points into rotor chamber. Triangular rotor shape. Maximum power: 280bhp (DIN) at 7000rpm.

Transmission: ZF five-speed all-synchromesh manual gearbox and single-dry-plate clutch, all in unit with hypoid-bevel final drive with limited slip feature. Engine ahead of line of rear wheels, and gearbox behind the line. Remote, centrally mounted gear change. Exposed, univerally jointed drive shafts to rear wheels.

Chassis: Pressed and fabricated platform-type chassis frame in sheet steel, topped by glass-fiber coupe body shell bonded and riveted to this frame. Independent front suspension by coil spring/damper units and wishbones. Independent rear suspension by coil spring/damper units, wishbones and radius arms. Telescopic dampers. Recirculating ball steering. Four-wheel hydraulically operated disk brakes, no servo. Bolt-on 14in cast-alloy road wheels. Tires: 195VR14in. Two-door "gull-wing" coupe-style two-seater bodywork.

Dimensions: Wheelbase: 8ft 7.1in (2.62m). Front track: 4ft 6.3in (1.38m), rear track: 4ft 5.9in (1.37m). Overall length: 13ft 10.5in (4.23m). Unladen weight: 2426lb (1100kg).

turbocharged V8 engine rated at 500bhp, and set up an absolute world record for lapping a closed circuit at no less than 250.97mph (403.81km/h).

All this activity, however, fell into the twin categories of high-speed research and product publicity and was rather divorced from the everyday activities of the company. In the meantime the evolution, launch, maturity and subsequent replacement of the various passenger cars was continuing at a great pace. It is possible to detail this process, and to see the way in which Daimler-Benz policy was progressing, but to make sense of it all the author hopes the reader will allow him to separate the engines story from that of the cars themselves.

It should be remembered that up to 1965 the mass-production Mercedes-Benz passenger-car range had all been built from one or other derivative of the be-finned four-door sedan body shells first seen in 1959, and that at that juncture a new large car had appeared to take over the upper segment of the range. This now left the smaller-engined cars with an aging unit-construction body style, and led observers to the assumption that there would always be two distinctly different styles—in size, shape and marketing scope—in the future.

This proved to be correct, and the first entirely new model to appear, early in 1968, was what Daimler-Benz most appropriately called its "New Generation" of cars. Not only were they all based on a rather smaller and more compact unit-construction body/chassis unit than the cars they replaced, but there were many new engineering features, and a great deal of obvious attention to the considerations of safety and protection of occupants. More than that, however, was the fact that there seemed to be so very many of them—even at first there were 15 separate models.

The body style of the four-door sedan shell—and of the smart two-door four-seater coupes and the long-wheelbase versions which evolved from it— was neat, smart, carefully rounded off and almost entirely predictable by Daimler-Benz standards. In every way it was a rather smaller version of the larger car which had been on sale since the end of 1965, and indeed one had to look very carefully at cars encountered on the open road before establishing which was which. This incidentally, caused one of the only bouts of customer petulance which Daimler-Benz encountered at the time, because once again there was the old "status" problem of owning a top-of-the-line 183.1cu in (3.0-liter) sedan which might, just, be mistaken for a more humble 122.0cu in (2.0-liter) diesel!

The main chassis change, and an important one in terms of its effect on future Daimler-Benz models, was that the traditional Mercedes-Benz swing-axle rear suspension had been abandoned in favor of a new system incorporating coil springs and semi-trailing wishbones. Even though the swing-axle layout had been progressively refined, modified and further complicated by such things as camber compensators and self-leveling struts, there was no escaping the fact that it was still possible for unfavorable wheel angles to develop, and for strange on-the-limit handling behavior to show up. The new semi-trailing layout, mounted on its own sub-frame, was similar in many ways to systems used by cars built by Triumph and BMW, and provided a very acceptable compromise between handling and ride, and its occupation of valuable space. To match the rear end, there was also a new coil-spring independent front suspension, notable for its massive pressed-steel cross-member, and for the very careful attention which had been paid to the insulation of the passenger compartment from noise and vibration at the road wheels.

Although, at first, there was only the one original body style—a four-door

The smallest car in the 1980/1981 Daimler-Benz company's range was the 200 sedan, recently fitted with new and efficient four-cylinder engines. This one basic body style accepted many different gasoline and diesel engines of four, five and six cylinders, up to 170.9cu in (2.8 liters).

This group of illustrations shows the careful attention to detail obvious in all aspects of modern Daimler-Benz styling and engineering. The car is a 1977 450SL fitted with the removable metal hardtop. There was also the option of a smaller-capacity V8 engine, and the long-wheelbase fixed-head version was either a 350SLC or a 450SLC.

sedan with a 108in (2.74m) wheelbase—it could be supplied with a variety of four-cylinder and six-cylinder gasoline engines in carefully graded sizes and power outputs between 122.0 and 152.6cu in (2.0 and 2.5 liters), and, of course, there were the diesel engine options without which the West German taxi trade would surely not have been able to stay in business! Although there was not a single new engine in this very comprehensive range—a fact more significant than was realized at the time—there had been a great deal of juggling of dimensions and modification to achieve an integrated Mercedes-Benz passenger car range starting from the low-powered and "small"-bodied 200D, and finishing with the "large"-bodied 300SEL.

This, however, was only the start. Within a few years, the full scope and nature of the technical revolution planned at Stuttgart for the 1970s began to become clear. First, in the fall of 1969, came an entirely new V8 engine [one which was quite different from the 384.4cu in (6.3-liter) design used in the 600 Limousines and Pullman models]; next, in the spring of 1971, came a brand-new range of coupes and convertibles to replace the elegant "pagoda-roof" 280SLs. To follow that, in the spring of 1972, another completely new engine— a six-cylinder unit—made its bow, and, in the fall of that year, the transformation was completed by the release of the magnificent "S" class sedans. The interrelation of one new car or of one new engine with another was extremely complex, and to a fascinated observer it had all the interest and challenge of a technological jig-saw puzzle. It showed, above all, that a great deal of thought and long-range planning had gone into the rejuvenation of the

whole range. A study of all these cars, which typified the Daimler-Benz approach to motoring in the 1970s, showed that it thought that if anything could be preferable to having the occupants surviving an accident, it was that the cars should not have the accident at all. In other words, the new breed of Mercedes-Benz models were not only very carefully built and included all manner of safety features, but they were also fast, splendidly braked and possessed of excellent handling and response.

Top left and right: Not until the late 1970s did the first Mercedes-Benz station wagon come on to the market. Called the "T-Wagen," it was based on the body shell and mechanical options of the smaller of the two Mercedes-Benz sedans.

Bottom left and right: At the end of the 1960s, one really needed a spotter's course to identify all the slightly different models. This was a 280SE 3.5 coupe, with a two-door conversion of the original S-class sedan shell, and a 213.6cu in (3.5-liter) V8 engine.

Since the complete five-year program hinged around the choice, the specification and the range of motive power provided, one ought to analyze what was done to provide modern engines. By the mid-1960s the existing range of four-cylinder and six-cylinder units, all interrelated by common tooling, common development, or merely by a common philosophy, was beginning to look old-fashioned and—worse—the "six" could not be stretched any further than the 170.9cu in (2.8 liters) it achieved in 1968. Daimler-Benz not only wanted to provide new and better engines in the markets it already covered, but wished to move very firmly up-market. In the 1960s the company was stuck at 170.9cu in (2.8 liters)—for the 1970s it wanted to meet the Americans head on, and wanted very powerful new designs of up to 274.6cu in (4.5 liters)!

The first new engine was the iron-block single-overhead-camshaft V8, made in two sizes—213.4cu in (3499cc) and, with a longer stroke, 275.8cu in (4520cc)—which made its debut in 1969. Like all modern up-market Daimler-Benz units, it had Bosch fuel injection, was neatly and meticulously engineered, and was intended for use in several different cars. It was a big heavy engine—no one denied that—but it proved to be not only extremely powerful, especially in 274.6cu in (4.5-liter) form, but extremely reliable. At first it found its way into the larger (and, in design terms, older) touring cars, but was an integral part of the design of the new sporting cars and the new large sedans.

That took care of the extension, upwards, of the engine range and, incidentally, it also neatly filled in the yawning gap between the largest of the six-cylinder units and the 384.4cu in (6.3-liter) V8 of the 600 models. Next, then, a tiny gap was plugged between the existing "six" and the new V8s, with the launch of a brand-new twin-overhead-camshaft six-cylinder unit of 167.5cu in (2746cc). Then, as now, nearly a decade later, there was only the one engine size and no derivatives; the engine could be supplied with Bosch fuel injection and 185bhp, or with Solex carburetion and 160bhp. Incidentally, although it was extremely close to the largest of the single-cam six-cylinder units in capacity [167.5cu in (2746cc) compared with 169.5cu in (2778cc)] it was entirely different in detail, and there was no common production-line tooling.

That took care of the hardware, the motive power, but in the meantime Daimler-Benz had done a great deal to satisfy its customers, particularly at home and in North America, by supplying some sumptuous, fast and prestigious new cars. At the end of the 1960s and in the early 1970s it should be remembered that there was a continuous flow of new legislation in the United States which not only sought to limit the exhaust emission of engines sold there, but made many new demands for safety equipment in the chassis and body structures. In reaction to this, many European manufacturers did not even attempt to cope, and ran down their North American sales efforts. Some, like Daimler-Benz, attacked the problem with great zeal and thoroughness, produced better and better cars, and increased their already-excellent reputations in the world's largest automobile market.

It was, unfortunately, inevitable that a new generation of cars would at once be less powerful, yet heavier, than their predecessors, and the new Daimler-Benz models were no exception to this trend. Perhaps, however, one was still surprised to see the sheer bulk and massive construction of the 350SL coupes and convertibles when they appeared in 1971. The cars they replaced, the svelte and feline 280SL models, had always looked quite small and, somehow, delicate, but there was no trace of this in the new cars. Furthermore, in accord with the latest Daimler-Benz approach to marketing, this was not just one new car, but a whole new range. Not only would there be open and closed versions of the style, but there would be two sizes of the newest V8 engine [and a rather

Left: The "New Generation" models of 1968 set Mercedes-Benz firmly on the path to technical supremacy in the 1970s. This was a six-cylinder 250 of 1973, but the range encompassed 122.0 to 170.9 cu in (2.0 to 2.8-liter) models.

Right: The final flowering of the 1972–80 S-class range was the 450SEL 6.9 model, which was the longer-wheelbase four-door sedan car shell mated to the immensely-powerful 721.0cu in (6.9-liter) V8 engine. The 450SEL (without 6.9 suffix) used the smaller-block 274.6cu in (4.5-liter) V8.

strangled 274.6cu in (4.5-liter) derivative for North America], a multitude of transmission options, and even a long-wheelbase close-coupled four-seater coupe development of the original two-seater style.

Naturally the unit-construction body/chassis unit was all new, and although the front and rear suspensions used major components from the "New Generation" touring cars they also used parts to be found on a later model not yet revealed.

The strategy started in 1968 was finally completed in the fall of 1972, when Daimler-Benz swept away the last of the old-generation swing-axle rear suspension cars, and ushered in its impressive "S" class sedans. Not even the most dedicated Mercedes-Benz enthusiasts had been expecting anything quite as sumptuous, quite as versatile, quite as outstanding as this. At one step, it seemed, Daimler-Benz had set the standard by which *every* other car in the world would have to be judged. The company made no secret of the fact that it wanted to have cars as fast and as enterprisingly engineered as the latest Jaguars (which range now included a V12 engined sedan) *and* of comparable

quality and longevity to the latest Rolls-Royce products.

Everything known about safety engineering, and the 70 accumulated years of passenger-car experience built up by Daimler and Benz, went into the new "S" class sedans. They were so quiet and refined, so roadworthy, so fast, and — as experience proved — so very reliable, that it was clearly going to be difficult to make dramatic improvements when the time comes to replace them.

In looks, the "S" class cars were merely up-dated versions of the modern Mercedes-Benz theme, and there was an obvious family resemblance to the "New Generation" cars. The unique Mercedes radiator was still in evidence, but had once again been slightly reshaped, the headlights were now faired into the integrated nose with great delicacy (and, for North America, a four-light system was specified), while the four-door body style was larger, subtly sleeker, and somehow more assertive than that of the "New Generation" cars.

As with the 350SL/450SL/450SLC sporting cars, the "S" class models also came in several varieties which included the choice of both "New Generation" engines, the "six" and the V8, and of a conventional or lengthened wheelbase.

Right in the middle of the fast, safe and immensely strong S-class cars of the 1970s was the 350SE sedan, with the shorter (though still spacious) of the two wheelbases, and the smallest, 213.6cu in (3.5-liter) V8 engine.

The 450SL was originally developed for North American sales – the larger 274.6cu in (4.5-liter) engine being needed to offset power losses due to limits imposed by exhaust emission "de-toxing," but later it became widely available all over the world.

Every detail of the modern Mercedes-Benz models styling, and the function of the equipment, has been worked out with great care.

It is likely that no other car-making concern takes quite so much trouble to approach technical perfection. This set of examples is from a modern 280E sedan.

The 280E sedan — complete with 170.9cu in (2.8-liter) twin-cam fuel-injected engine — is the standard in Europe and North America by which so many other cars are judged.

The one departure from tradition was that no coachbuilt convertible or coupe body styles were offered, and indeed this form of indulgence seems to have disappeared from the scene at Sindelfingen.

They were cars without which, it seemed, no self-respecting industrialist, country gentleman, or even film star or personality could afford to do without. If the Hollywood motoring scenes of the 1960s had been littered with Jaguars, it was now the larger Mercedes-Benz models which began to make their appearance.

One would think that after such a burst of technological and marketing

Above : One of the many derivatives of the "New Generation" models of the early 1970s was this 146.7cu in (2.4-liter) diesel-engined 240D, very popular indeed in countries where the price of diesel fuel was much lower than that of gasoline.

Right : The least expensive version of the S-class cars of the 1970s was the 280SE, which had a twin-cam six-cylinder engine of 170.9cu in (2.8-liters).

Left : The 230TE station wagon combined all the elegance and practicality of the sedans, with the load-carrying capability of a station wagon. In this, as in so many other aspects of motoring, Daimler-Benz set new standards in the late 1970s.

Right : For the 1980s the 350SL/450SLC models were given a new generation of light-alloy V8 engines (which they shared with the latest S-class cars), becoming the 380SLs and 500SLCs.

activity, Daimler-Benz would merely rest on its laurels and reap the benefits in the years which followed. The firm might have been tempted to do so, but showed no signs of lethargy, and the shattering effect of the Israel-Egypt "Suez" war of 1973 made it certain that they never would. One immediate effect was that Daimler-Benz engineers began to look around for ways to lighten the cars, and to make them more fuel-efficient, and another was that they forged ahead with their search for alternative power plants and applications.

Slotting the twin-cam 164.8cu in (2.7-liter) six-cylinder engine into the 350SL's structure was certainly a "down-market" reaction to Suez, but the arrival of a *five*-cylinder diesel engine was not. The fact that it was launched in 1974 could not have been more timely, but that had been planned for some time—the five-cylinder in-line layout, incidentally, was a world "first" for a maker of passenger cars. The "five" was admittedly no more than a derivative of the existing four-cylinder 240D in technical terms, and it could only just be squeezed into the engine bay of the "New Generation" cars; the real achievement was in being able to provide acceptable balance and refinement, and in

Left: The "New S-class" models – really the third generation of large prestige models which originated in the mid-1960s – were launched in 1979, and will carry on at least until the end of the 1980s. Though they look superficially like the superseded 1972–1980 models, their body style was subtly reprofiled to improve the aerodynamic performance.

1980 Type 500SEL "S" Class Sedan

Engine: Eight cylinders, in 90 degree "V" formation, in five-bearing light-alloy combined block/crankcase. Bore and stroke, capacity: 3.80×3.35in, 303.4cu in (96.5× 85mm, 4973cc). Detachable light-alloy cylinder heads. Two overhead valves per cylinder, in line along each bank of cylinders, operated by single overhead camshaft per bank, with interposed finger-type rockers with hydraulic adjustment. Bosch indirect fuel injection, into inlet ports. Maximum power: 240bhp (DIN) at 4750rpm.

Transmission: Daimler-Benz four-speed automatic transmission, incorporating torque convertor, in unit with front-mounted engine. Remote, centrally mounted gearchange. Open propeller shaft to chassis-mounted hypoid-bevel final drive. Exposed, universally jointed drive shafts to rear wheels.

Chassis: Unit construction pressed-steel body/chassis unit, with some light-alloy panels. Independent front suspension by coil springs and wishbones. Independent rear suspension by coil springs and semi-trailing wishbones; optional hydraulic self-leveling control. Telescopic dampers. Recirculating ball steering with power assistance. Four-wheel hydraulically operated disk brakes with vacuum servo assistance. Bolt-on 14in pressed steel disk wheels. Tires: 205/70VR14in. Four-door sedan bodywork.

Dimensions: Wheelbase: 10ft 1.6in (3.09m). Front track: 5ft 0.8in (1.54m), rear track: 4ft 11.7in (1.52m). Overall length: 16ft 10.1in (5.13m). Unladen weight: 3640lb (1651kg).

extending the company's range of diesels without enormous financial investment. It was not, of course, the first-ever in-line five-cylinder engine—such layouts had been used in trucks for some years—nor, it seems, will it be the last, for Audi produced its own gasoline-powered "five" a few years later, at which point Rover rather proudly admitted that it had been considering the same sort of thing in the mid-1960s. Nothing, however, should obliterate the fact that here, as in the use of anti-lock braking, gull-wing doors, self-leveling suspension, and many other features, Daimler-Benz was truly a world leader.

It was altogether typical of the West German concern, incidentally, that it was not merely content to market a five-cylinder diesel on its own, for in due course it also began to sell a turbocharged derivative (first in the United States) which was not only much more powerful than the normally aspirated engine, but was also remarkably "clean" in terms of exhaust emissions. At Stuttgart and Sindelfingen there is certainly never a lull in technical activity.

Even though in the aftermath of the Suez war fuel prices soared and continued to increase throughout the 1970s, the demand for Mercedes-Benz cars never faltered. More than 300,000 cars were sold for the first time in 1972,

The S-class car for the 1980s, available with a choice of wheelbase lengths and three engines – a 170.9cu in (2.8-liter) six, 231.9cu in (3.8-liter) and 305.1cu in (5.0-liter) V8s – are in the eyes of many experts the best cars in the world.

the 350,000 mark was reached in 1975, and more than 400,000 cars were sold in 1977. With very little variation throughout the decade, Daimler-Benz always managed to export between 44 and 50 percent of all those cars. But motoring habits, and motoring fashions, had changed. Manufacturers as famous as Daimler-Benz no longer went in for "follies" or self-indulgent models; it might mean, therefore, that the new and latest cars were no longer as visually sensational as they had been in the past, and that motoring writers were no longer as lyrical in their descriptions, but it could never detract from the remarkably consistent improvements which continued to be made.

What has happened at Daimler-Benz in the last few years is a perfect example of this. To look at the product line-up on offer as the 80th anniversary of the birth of the Mercedes car approaches is to see cars superficially like those of the early 1970s. The truth, however, is rather different. Not only have the "New Generation" cars been replaced by a different, type W123 range (which includes a new in-line single-cam six-cylinder engine and—since 1980—new four-cylinder engines intended for more versatile use in the 1980s), but the wonderfully successful "S" class cars have been replaced by new "S" class models offering more safety, better fuel economy, better aerodynamics and even further improved safety facilities. The coupes have been improved by fitting them, and the new "S" class cars, with light-alloy V8 engines which are, at one and the same time, lighter, more fuel efficient *and* more powerful.

The way in which the "S" class cars were reshaped, re-engineered and rehoned for the 1980s, while retaining a body style so similar to the superseded cars that one needs several looks to be convinced, is indicative of the way all modern engineers are having to work for the stringent-fuel expensive-motoring era of the future.

Compared with the old W116 models, the new W126 range for the 1980s has bodies with slightly longer wheelbases, but with 2in narrower widths. New cars' noses are even more smoothly detailed than before, and are slightly nearer the ground, while the luggage compartment lid level is higher than before and the shell weight has been reduced by 110lb. The drag coefficient, checked out in several wind-tunnels, has been reduced from 0.41 to 0.36, which does not sound too dramatic until it is translated as a 12 percent improvement. The new light-alloy V8 engines are not only 100lb lighter than the original iron-block units, but are also rather more powerful. All-in-all, there is an overall fuel saving of about ten percent. What is extremely encouraging and is perhaps of great importance even at this early stage is that traditional Mercedes-Benz customers appear to have realized what has been done, why it was necessary to do it, and thoroughly approve of it.

In the next few years, there is every reason to think that Daimler-Benz's activities will continue to develop in the same logical way. The importance of the tightening North American "fleet average" fuel consumption figures has not been missed, and this will certainly mean that the Mercedes-Benz cars of the 1980s will be more economical *and* physically smaller than they are today. Already, sneak pictures of a rumored "small" Mercedes-Benz model have appeared in the motoring press, and it is widely expected that the small engines revealed in 1980 will find their true vocation in these cars.

The advances made by Daimler-Benz to its cars in the last 20 years have been quite astonishing, and it is certain that the same sort of progress will be made in the future. At the beginning of this chapter, the author suggested that Daimler-Benz management set out in the 1960s to build the best cars in the world in the 1970s. Perhaps this has already been achieved? One thing seems certain—that Daimler-Benz, and no other automobile manufacturing concern, will be setting every standard in the 1980s.

9. THE OTHER FACE OF DAIMLER-BENZ

In 1978 when I spent six weeks traveling around South America watching the Mercedes-Benz 450SLC coupes dominate a marathon rally, I saw evidence of the three-pointed star just about everywhere. It was not merely that the Daimler-Benz rally service network was so comprehensive, but it seemed that on most occasions when I took a coach from airport to city center, or encountered a truck in the steamy Brazilian jungle, high in the mountains of Bolivia or in the barren wilderness of the Argentinian pampas, the Daimler-Benz insignia would be displayed on the nose of the vehicle.

Those of us who are out-and-out motoring enthusiasts tend to forget that there is another very important face to Daimler-Benz. The passenger cars have been so glamorous and so successful for so many years that the building of trucks, buses, delivery vans, four-wheel-drive machines, stationary power units and aero-engines is often ignored. But to do this is to distort the entire Daimler-Benz picture. One simple but basic statistic, lifted from the company's *1979 Annual Report*, makes this very clear. In that year more than 422,000 cars were built, which was an all-time record, but in the same period no fewer than 256,467 commercial vehicles accompanied them. In business terms—in the amount of financial turnover generated—the commercial vehicle side is *the* most important Daimler-Benz activity.

Commercial vehicle production in the modern Daimler-Benz is diversified, not only throughout West Germany, but all over the world. Although the

Previous page: One of many interesting public service vehicles built by Daimler-Benz since the Second World War is this front-engined bus, built in the 1950s. Daimler-Benz now build more buses and trucks than any other manufacturer in Europe.

Surely one of the earliest of all engine-powered fire engines in the world was this one, built by Daimler in 1896.

20568

company's passenger car assembly is centered on the Sindelfingen factory, southwest of Stuttgart, there are several commercial vehicle assembly facilities in Germany, the largest of which is at Worth near Karlsruhe. In complete contrast to the passenger cars, however, Daimler-Benz trucks are also produced (not merely assembled from parts sent out from Germany, but manufactured, with local material, local tooling, and separate facilities) in other countries—notably in Brazil and Argentina.

For a historian, the bright modern bustle of activity at Worth, where most of the company's large commercial vehicles are built, is misleading. Worth was a "green-field" site, bought in 1960, starting production in 1965, and still undergoing expansion. Nowhere, not in the lines of the trucks themselves, nor in the architecture of the buildings, is there any evidence of the company's proud heritage. Yet it is a fact that both Daimler and Benz, when their companies were still very small, were already able and prepared to build working machines as well as private cars.

Daimler's first fire engine was in use by 1888, when no more than a handful of any make of car had been built, and his first trucks followed in the 1890s. Benz began building buses in the mid-1890s. Since then there have been so many important developments that it is difficult to note the milestones. One should not, however, ignore the arrival of the first Daimler airplane engines (1901), the world's first application of the diesel engine to a road vehicle (in 1924, for Benz trucks), the use of fuel-injection for aero-engines (in the mid-1930s), the arrival of the four-wheel-drive Unimog in 1948, and the carefully planned rationalized range of trucks introduced in the mid- and late 1960s.

While Daimler and Benz were still separate concerns, they competed on several fronts. It was only after the merger of 1926 that rationalization began, and it was the centralization of passenger-car production at Stuttgart which allowed all truck assembly to be concentrated at the original Benz factory at Mannheim, and at Gaggenau. But all this is to run ahead of the historical story which will now be summarized.

Looking very little larger than a full-size car was this Benz bus of 1895.

Because Benz was the original pioneer of motor vehicles (but only by a few months, as has already been noted) I will trace his interests in non-passenger car activity first. It all began in 1895 when his first omnibus, looking very much like a stagecoach from which the horses and reins had escaped, was developed from the eight-seater Landau car; two of this type were put into service from the town of Siegen. Although they were not a success, they were followed in the early 1900s by front-engined trucks which still retained Benz's traditional (and by now old-fashioned) belt drive.

In the meantime, the Wright brothers had ushered in the age of the airplane, and in 1912 the German Kaiser offered prizes for the best German airplane engines. Although there were 26 competitors for this prize, Benz gained the award for four-cylinder engines with a 100bhp design; this did not, however, lead to military orders, and a six-cylinder design soon followed.

In the meantime, Benz had taken over a factory at Gaggenau, originally set up in 1893, and one which had at one time built a car known as the Lilliput. The Bergmann concern who owned Gaggenau concentrated on trucks and buses, and it was the takeover, in 1910, of this business which allowed Benz to diversify rapidly into commercial vehicles up to 6.6 tons (6000kg). Even after the 1926 merger, Gaggenau has continued to specialize in the manufacture of

Essential supplies! A beer delivery truck, built by Daimler in 1903 and used by a British brewery.

commercial, public service and agricultural vehicles.

By the 1920s, too, lengthy development work on diesel engines came to fruition. It was Benz engineers who evolved the pre-combustion layout, which truly became feasible when fuel injection apparatus became available after the First World War. In February 1924 a Benz five-ton truck was first shown, with a 50hp diesel engine, and it was this basic design which really gave the combine a great advantage over its competitors at the end of the 1920s.

Daimler, for his part, began by trying to apply his high-speed gasoline engines to various machines, including motorboats, streetcars and even to an airship. It was this last application which brought Daimler to the attention of Count Zeppelin, who forged links with him which were to last 40 years. By the 1890s, too, Daimler's so-called stationary engines had also been applied to small locomotives, large streetcars, and to other machines—the first assault on North America came in the same period.

In 1896 Daimler and Maybach had evolved the first Daimler truck, still with an under-floor rear engine and with belt drive. By the end of the century Daimler was matching Benz in most fields, including that of airship-engine manufacture, and had built buses from 1898. An agreement with Motor-fahrzeud und Motorenfabrik Berlin (in the 1890s) led to Daimler absorbing the

Above A 1901 Benz truck, powered by a 4.5hp engine – surely not powerful enough to carry a sizeable payload.

Right: A 1917 20/40hp Daimler truck, carrying a familiar address.

Bottom right: This truck was placarded to commemorate the first 10 years of diesel-engined truck production by Daimler and Benz.

Marienfelde factory in Berlin in 1902. Thereafter Berlin looked after Daimler's commercial vehicle interests, while passenger-car building was concentrated at Stuttgart. By the end of the 19th century, too, the Austrian Daimler concern had been set up in Vienna, where commercial-vehicle design and construction was always a major part of activities.

Daimler introduced the first mail-bus, in Bavaria, in 1905, and in 1912 they also competed successfully for one of the Kaiser's aero-engine prizes, in this case for a six-cylinder engine. The "Mercedes" marque title was soon adopted for the aero-engines, and in the 1914–1918 War engines of up to eight cylinders with 230hp were successfully built in quantity. In the meantime Daimler had been working on diesel engines for some time, and its first saleable products were marine and stationary units. As far as truck installations were concerned, Daimler were almost neck and neck with Benz, as it showed diesel-powered trucks and buses at the Berlin show in the fall of 1923, and deliveries began shortly afterwards.

After the original association between Daimler and Benz was agreed in 1924 (still not a full-blooded merger, however), duplication of commercial vehicle manufacture was abandoned. Daimler adopted the Benz pre-combustion chamber invention, and assembly of trucks was concentrated at Gaggenau, Marienfelde being reduced to a supplier of components. This all happened at a time of incredibly high inflation in Germany, when trade was obviously severely affected. It was not until the full and final fusion of Daimler with Benz, effected in 1926, that the true benefits of rationalization began to become obvious.

In the next ten years or more, Daimler-Benz's two principal non-passenger-car efforts were in commercial-vehicle and aero-engine manufacture. With the rapid modernization of trucks and buses throughout the world, which was also

Right: By 1926 Daimler and Benz had just merged. This was their typical double decker bus of the period. It could carry 60 people.

Below: Even in the 1930s when international relations were somewhat ticklish, French concerns sometimes bought Mercedes-Benz trucks. This one had a payload of 8.5 metric tonnes.

linked with the inexorable rise to domination of the diesel engine, there is really no need to detail the changes. There were multi-axle and four-wheel-drive chassis before the end of the 1930s, and the bus market also began to turn more and more to acceptance of the group's offerings.

In the 1930s, however, it was the development and production of the remarkable DB600 series aero-engines which took most of the limelight. It is a fact that most of the great air battles of the Second World War involved the use of two very famous V12 engines—the Rolls-Royce Merlin design, and the famous "inverted" V12 developed by Daimler-Benz. Both engines started their service lives with modest power outputs (modest, that is, by later aviation standards), and both more than doubled their capabilities in the next ten years.

The original DB600 of 1935 evolved from an earlier engine (the F2) which had been used in high-speed motorboats. It was a water-cooled engine, with 12 cylinders in "inverted" 60-degree "V" formation—which is to say that the crankshaft line was at the top of the engine, and the two banks of cylinders, in 60-degree "V" formation, were below it. It was, in every way, a logical layout, for it allowed the crankshaft to be in direct alignment with the propeller, the fuselage profile to be slimmed down in front of the pilots' line of sight, and the exhaust gases to be extracted from the cowling at a low level. Naturally it was supercharged, and there was automatic boost regulation to compensate for the change in atmospheric densities at various operating heights.

In its original form, with a 5.9in (150mm) cylinder bore and a stroke of 6.3in (160mm), the 2068.6cu in (33.9-liter) DB600 produced 1050hp at 2400rpm. Although its first and most famous application was in the famous Messerschmidt Me109 single-seater fighter plane, the derivatives of the engine were later applied to several other Luftwaffe airframes. Like the Rolls-Royce

Merlin engine, it was an astonishingly versatile power plant, and soon attracted a formidable reputation. Indeed it would be fair to say that this engine, and another series of designs from BMW, did much to keep the Luftwaffe airborne in the next critical years.

As with all famous fighting engines, however, the DB600 design was only a beginning. In the next few years, not only was the capacity pushed up to no less than 2727.6cu in (44.7 liters) by means of increases to the bore *and* the stroke, but the carburetion system was replaced by fuel injection, a diesel-powered version was developed, and there was even a gargantuan installation of coupled (DB605A) V12s which effectively formed a twin-crankshaft V24, had a capacity of 4356.8cu in (71.4 liters), and produced a maximum of 3000hp!

The normal gasoline-powered V12 received a great deal of attention from development engineers in the next few years. By 1941, and when slightly enlarged to 2178.4cu in (35.7 liters), it had become the DB605, and produced

Below: The type 03 500 six-cylinder (diesel-engined) 90hp bus produced between 1949 and 1955. It could carry 60 people.

1500hp, while in 1942 a further version, the 2727.6cu in (44.7-liter) DB603, was rated at 1750hp. In the same year the diesel-powered derivative, the DB607, also of 2727.6cu in (44.7 liters), was rated at 1750hp, and found applications in aircraft and in marine installations. By the end of the conflict, in 1945, the most powerful and highly developed engine in this family was the DB603L of 2727.6cu in (44.7 liters) which, with a sophisticated form of methanol/water injection, was rated at no less than 2400hp.

It is worth recalling, too, that the sensational Type 80 Land Speed Record car project of 1939/1940 was to have chased its 400mph (644km/h) target with the help of a 1750hp DB603 aero-engine. No one, it seems, doubted that this was the ideal power plant for the job.

After the holocaust of 1939–1945 had come to an end, Daimler-Benz had to abandon its production of aero-engines, and was faced with an enormously daunting job of getting its non-passenger car factories back into use. It was, indeed, the first priority, as the need for all kinds of transport vehicles was more important to West Germany (by now partitioned) than was that for passenger cars.

Surprisingly enough, the Mannheim factory (which included the original Benz buildings) had suffered relatively little damage, though the Gaggenau factory, which had been looking after all truck final assembly for some years, was virtually in ruins. There was effectively nothing left of the Marienfelde factory in Berlin, and what *did* remain was speedily confiscated by the Russians and whisked away to an Iron Curtain country.

First, however, Daimler-Benz management began to get things going once again by intensifying the service, repair and rebuilding facilities in its factories and, as these were progressively rebuilt, the company began to think about producing new models. Apart from new trucks and public service vehicles, Daimler-Benz decided to enter a completely new market sector — and in 1948 its secret labors were revealed. At the first postwar Frankfurt Agricultural Show, the firm showed the "Universales Motorgerat," a vehicle soon affectionately known as a "Unimog." Here, for the first time from Daimler-Benz, was a four-wheel-drive multi-purpose machine which could be a tractor, an agricultural prime-mover, or a transporter of men and materials, and one

Below right: The versatile four-wheel-drive Unimog is still with us. This was one of the first (1951) models – built at the old Benz works at Gaggenau.

The Daimler-Benz headquarters factory at Stuttgart-Unterturkheim with a portion of the test track visible in the right foreground.

Built on virgin territory in the 1960s, the Worth plant is now the center of Daimler-Benz heavy truck manufacture.

which could clamber over, through, or around, almost every type of terrain. Daimler-Benz, like Rover in Britain, had noted the versatility and popularity of the Jeeps used by Allied troops in the Second World War, and had applied its own solution to the same design criteria.

Series production began at Gaggenau in 1948 and has continued ever since. In more than 30 years, of course, Unimogs have been built in many different versions with gasoline or diesel engines and are still as versatile as ever.

Apart from the continuous development of new models and of the widening of the range, much of the postwar Daimler-Benz commercial vehicle story hinges around the expansion, rationalization and modernization of factories. Faint-hearted economists would, no doubt, question the wisdom of the Daimler-Benz policy in allocating final assembly of certain vehicles and ranges to particular factories, rather than lumping the whole business together into one vast plant, but management has always believed, very strongly, that each group of workers needs to have a sense of personal identification. Although it is a fact that most factories supply components or complete assemblies to other locations, it is usually arranged for one van, one truck, or one coach chassis assembly line to be in use there as well.

Much of the postwar expansion of the Daimler-Benz commercial vehicle activity has come from the absorbtion of existing factories into the group, though one brand-new factory—at Worth—has also been built. This process started with the take-over of Hanomag Henschel in 1949, whose business had been founded in 1810 and whose Kassel factory had built Hanomag cars from 1924 to 1939 and trucks from 1925.

Next, and far-reaching as far as the entire West German motor industry was concerned, was the Daimler-Benz link with the Auto-Union group which lasted only from 1956 to 1964. Not only did it involve Daimler-Benz ownership of another car manufacturer, but it eventually brought yet another factory into the modern Daimler-Benz empire.

The story began in the mid-1950s when Daimler-Benz was once again prosperous and was looking for a means to expand and to widen its range of

The Mercedes-Benz "G-Wagen," a four-wheel-drive vehicle built since 1979 at the Steyr-Daimler-Puch factory in Austria, and sold with a variety of diesel and gasoline engines.

passenger cars. The ideal way, but one which would have taken up a great deal of time and money, was to design new smaller cars and build new factories in which to have them made. This was rejected; instead, an agreed bid was made for control of the Auto-Union group of companies, whose DKW cars were being built at the re-established Dusseldorf factory, and whose trucks were being built at Ingolstadt, north of Stuttgart. Auto-Union, at the time, though consisting of several famous old marques including Audi and Horch, were only building two-stroke DKWs.

Under Daimler-Benz control and with the help of the engineers and stylists, a program of modernization was carried out. Not only did Auto-Union benefit from the help given in styling a new car (initially revealed in 1963 as the Auto-Union F102), and from an entirely new four-stroke four-cylinder engine slotted into the F102 which became the Audi 60/75/90 range, but car production became concentrated at Ingolstadt, while the older Dusseldorf factory was hived off for Daimler-Benz use.

The end to this particular phase in the development of Daimler-Benz came in 1964, when management rethought its future policy, held discussions with the giant VW organization, and agreed to establish joint ownership of Auto-Union with VW putting in a great deal of new finance and taking over the running of the Ingolstadt factory. By 1968 VW had converted this partnership into full ownership, but late that year the last influence of Daimler-Benz on the Ingolstadt concern was revealed, when the Audi 100 was announced. Not only did that car retain the Daimler-Benz-designed four-cylinder engine, but it also featured a body style which had quite obviously come from Stuttgart as well. The Audi 100, initially a credit to Daimler-Benz, became something of an irritant in later years, for the Audi 100 was almost a direct competitor of the smallest and cheapest versions of the Mercedes-Benz "New Generation" models.

The last of the Daimler-Benz factories to be taken over from previous owners was the one at Bremen in the north of the Federal Republic. The factory had built its first cars in 1906 (Lloyds), and had proceeded through a series of mergers to build Hansa-Lloyds and Hansas. Carl Borgward took control at the end of the 1920s and produced the first Borgward car there in 1939. In the 1940s and 1950s the company and the factory were expanded rapidly, but Borgward overstretched itself and failed financially in 1961. Daimler-Benz eventually stepped in, in partnership with Hanomag-Henschel, and is now making Bremen

Bottom left: One of the many applications for specially equipped Unimog chassis – in use by the town of Mannheim.

famous as the Mercedes-Benz "satellite" producer of passenger cars—the first product being the popular T-Wagen station wagons of 1978.

All of these acquisitions, however, are dwarfed by the company's enterprise in developing the site at Worth from a green field, a pasture, which was none too dry and which needed extensive draining and reconstruction even before factory buildings could be erected. It all came about because the postwar demand for Daimler-Benz commercial vehicles was insatiable. Statistics, they say, are always boring, but one or two isolated quotations tell a very vivid story in this case. It has already been mentioned that, by tremendous efforts, it had

Below: The versatile Mercedes-Benz trucks of the 1970s were used for many jobs, and with many different bodies. This 26-tonne machine had a 256hp V8 diesel engine, or a 320hp V10 engine, and had a three-axle chassis.

Modern 1980-model examples of the big and comfortable Mercedes-Benz trucks and buses. By this time, an assembly facility had been opened up in North America, using parts supplied from Brazil.

been possible to build more than 5000 passenger cars in 1948, but in some ways this achievement was dwarfed by the building of 4773 trucks and associated vehicles, which were financially *and* commercially more valuable. Within twenty years, the production of cars had risen to more than 210,000, while the equivalent figure for trucks was 73,000. In the next 12 years, which brings the story up to 1980, that car production figure had been doubled again, while total commercial vehicle production had gone up more than three times.

As the postwar years passed by, the range of Daimler-Benz vehicles continued to increase. At first there was a rather restricted range of normal-control trucks and buses, plus the Unimog. By the 1950s, however, rear-engined buses were being built at Mannheim, and the range of trucks being built at a rebuilt Gaggenau factory included those with a payload of up to eight tons. Still, however, there was no end to the demand. Not only did it seem to Daimler-Benz directors that they could, and should, build heavier and heavier trucks, larger and larger buses and coaches, but also that they should get into the light delivery van "transporter" market.

With the help of Hanomag-Henschel, with whom Daimler-Benz was now in partnership, and after the upheaval caused by the building of the entirely new and spacious factory at Worth, Daimler-Benz soon found itself not only with the space in which to build the vehicles, but with a very wide range of products and a demand which continued to expand. The group now builds commercial vehicles of one type or another at every important juncture between two and 42 tons (two and 38 tonnes). The small "transporters," from two to four tons

An interesting half-way house introduced by Mercedes-Benz in 1980 : buses with normal rubber tires and suspensions, running in guided concrete tracks – urban "trains." The first demonstrations had been in Hamburg in 1979, but the system, for city use, was first installed in Essen.
Previous page: The Mercedes-Benz Courte-Paille U-1700 L competing in the 1982 Paris–Algiers–Dakar Rally.

(or tonnes), are assembled at Bremen in the same factory which also assembles T-Wagen passenger station wagons (and which will, reputedly, also assemble the much-rumored "small" Mercedes-Benz model from 1982 or 1983). Those in the four- to seven-ton (four- to six-tonne) range (a very popular and very specialized market sector) are assembled at Dusseldorf. Bus and coach assembly —more than 8500 were built in 1979—is concentrated at Mannheim, while Gaggenau continues to build Unimogs, and Worth looks after two distinct ranges of truck chassis spanning eight to 42 tons (seven to 38 tonnes). To feed them, other satellite factories supply engines, transmissions and steering gear.

These satellites also supply a large number of overseas assembly facilities, which are not to be confused with the Daimler-Benz factories which actually produce trucks from locally made components. Daimler-Benz is particularly proud of its two truck- and bus-building works in Brazil and in Argentina which have no imported components at all. The Brazil factory, for example, built more than 12,000 buses in 1979—more than the number actually built in West Germany in the same period.

Even as the 1980s open, further exciting commercial vehicle developments are being revealed. The heavy vehicles were completely rejuvenated in the early 1970s (these are the shapely forward-control trucks built at Worth) and the Type O 303 bus chassis followed in the mid-1970s. The Bremen-built light vans were new in 1977. Among the really new products, however, are the famous "bendy" buses, which are really buses and trailers in which the power plant is located in the trailer itself, and the intriguing new application of basic rail technology to the use of buses in confined spaces. This, the "O-Bahn" system, was first put into limited public service in Essen in 1980. Specially modified buses are guided by concrete "rails" and side rails, and the buses themselves have small sideways-facing guidance wheels which make contact with these rails. In Essen, too, where the route incorporates tunnels, the buses themselves are dual-powered with normal diesel engines and with electric traction which can be switched in or out of operation by the driver.

Although the Worth factory is now fighting for the title of "largest truck factory in the world" with the General Motors plant in North America—it can, after all, produce up to 100,000 chassis a year, and is already bursting at the seams—one of the more exciting developments in the next few years may be the expansion of a new truck assembly plant at Hampton, Virginia in the United States. Although its initial capacity is only 6000 chassis in the 11- to 15-ton (ten- to 14-tonne) range at first (CKD supplies come from the Daimler-Benz truck factory in Brazil), there is great scope for the future. This is truly a case of carrying the battle to the enemy, with a vengeance.

Obviously there is more, much more, to the Daimler-Benz range of activities, which can be no more than mentioned in a book of this length. It can all be summed up, however, by the fact that in 1979 the corporation's total sales were 27.4 thousand million Deutschmarks—more than $14,000 million, or more than £6500 million, based on exchange rates current at the time. Apart from the comprehensive domestic network of production factories, in the rest of the world there are 12 production plants, two licensed plants, and a further 24 locations where assembly from CKD packs (and, sometimes, a mix of CKD and home-manufactured parts) takes place. There are more than 4250 sales and service outlets in the world. A study of almost every major trend graph in the company's financial report—whether it is of production, of financial turnover, or of numbers employed—shows steady but inexorable growth.

It is no wonder that the three-pointed star and the name of Daimler-Benz have come to symbolize meticulous engineering and painstaking development. Nothing, it seems, is ever too much trouble for Daimler-Benz.

ACKNOWLEDGMENTS—

The Publishers would like to thank the following for their help in the preparation of this book: Mercedes-Benz (UK Limited; Coys of Kensington for photographs of some of the many fine cars which have passed through their hands; Mr & Mrs John Cupwell of the Mercedes-Benz Club who have given up their time to read the text; and Gerald Coward, the Chairman of the Club, who has kindly provided the Foreword. Many of the cars have been specially photographed by John Adams ARPS AIIP and the cooperation of individual owners has been much appreciated.

JOHN ADAMS half title, 7, 8/9, 25, 27 (all five), 28/29 (all five), 34, 42/43 (all four), 44/45 (all three), 60/61, 70, 72/73 (all four), 92/93, 108/109 (all three), 116/117, 122/128 (both), 124 (both), 125, 126 (both), 127 (both), 128/129 (all three), 132/133 (both), 134/135 (all three), 142 (both), 143, 156/157 (both), 180/181 (all four), 182 (both), 183 (both), 190 (both), 212/213, 218/219

NATIONAL MOTOR MUSEUM 4/5, 84/85

MERCEDES-BENZ (UK) LTD 10/11, 12, 13 (both), 14, 15, 18, 19 (both), 24, 31, 32/33 (lower), 36, 46/47, 49, 54/55, 95, 97 (both), 98, 99, 102/103 (both), 104/105 (both), 106/107 (all three), 110/111 (both), 112/113, 114, 119, 130/131 (all three), 138/139 (all three), 144, 146/147, 149, 150/151, 152, 153, 158/159, 155 (both), 158/159 (both), 163, 164/165 (both), 166/167, 168/169, 172/173 (all three), 175, 177 (both), 188/189 (all five), 191 (both), 192 (both), 193 (both), 194, 195 (both), 196/197 (all five), 200/ 201, 202, 203, 204/205 (all four), 206/207 (both), 208, 209, 210 (both), 211, 214/215 (both), 216/217, 220.

COYS OF KENSINGTON LTD 22/23, 32/33 (top), 41 (both), 50/51 (all three), 53 (both), 57, 64/65 (all four), 66 (all three), 67 (both), 68 (both), 69 (all three), 71, 74 (all three), 75 (all three), 78, 80 (all three), 83 (all three), 87 (both), 88 (both), 89, 90 (all three), 94, 137 (all four).

P. M. ALEXANDER 26.

MIRCO DECET 38/39, 120/121 (all three), 140/141 (all four), 170/171 (all six), 178/179 (all five), 184/185 (all four), 186/187 (all four).

LEN THORPE 30.

CRAVEN FOUNDATION 58.

R. T. BURRELL 76 (all four).

J. A. CONANT 77.

RAINER SCHLEGELMILCH/ OCTOPUS BOOKS front cover, 16–17, 20–21, 96–7.